A Pocket
Tour™ of Law
on the
Internet

Michael Gross

San Francisco • Paris • Düsseldorf • Soest

SYBEX

Pocket Tour concept:	Brenda Kienan
Acquisitions Manager:	Kristine Plachy
Acquisition and Developmental Editor:	Brenda Kienan
Editor:	Doug Robert
Technical Editors:	Juli Geiser Karen Helde
Book Designer:	Emil Yanos
Desktop Publisher:	Thomas Goudie
Production Assistant:	Kim Askew-Qasem
Indexer:	Ted Laux
Cover Designer:	Joanna Gladden
Cover Illustrator:	Mike Miller

Pocket Tour is a trademark of SYBEX Inc.

SYBEX is a registered trademark of SYBEX Inc.

TRADEMARKS: SYBEX has attempted throughout this book to distinguish proprietary trademarks from descriptive terms by following the capitalization style used by the manufacturer.

Every effort has been made to supply complete and accurate information. However, SYBEX assumes no responsibility for its use, nor for any infringement of the intellectual property rights of third parties which would result from such use.

Photographs and illustrations used in this book have been downloaded from publicly accessible file archives and are used in this book for news reportage purposes only to demonstrate the variety of graphics resources available via electronic access. The source of each photograph or illustration is identified. Text and images available over the Internet may be subject to copyright and other rights owned by third parties. Online availability of text and images does not imply that they may be reused without the permission of rights holders, although the Copyright Act does permit certain unauthorized reuse as fair use under 17 U.S.C. Section 107. Care should be taken to ensure that all necessary rights are cleared prior to reusing material distributed over the Internet. Information about reuse rights is available from the institutions who make their materials available over the Internet.

This publication is designed to provide information regarding its subject matter. It is sold with the understanding that the publisher and author are not engaged in rendering legal or other professional services. If legal advice or expert assistance is required, the services of a competent professional should be sought.

Copyright © 1995 SYBEX Inc., 2021 Challenger Drive, Alameda, CA 94501. World rights reserved. No part of this publication may be stored in a retrieval system, transmitted, or reproduced in any way, including but not limited to photocopy, photograph, magnetic or other record, without the prior agreement and written permission of the publisher.

Library of Congress Card Number: 95-70854
ISBN: 0-7821-1792-9

Manufactured in the United States of America
10 9 8 7 6 5 4 3 2 1

Acknowledgments

This book, like any other, is really a collective effort, and I am much indebted to the following people:

To Brenda Kienan, developmental editor, for the opportunity to write this book and because she is a pleasure to work with.

To Sharon Crawford, for her friendship, good advice, and not least for her contributions to this book.

To attorneys Paul Almanza, Dave Beck, Daniel Dienst, Anne Lackey, Joe Liburt, Jon Shanberge, and not least Ray Wierciszewski, all generous with their time and good counsel.

To Charlie Russel and Dan Tauber, for their vast technical know-how and their willingness to share it.

To Doug Robert for his fine editing of the manuscript, Juli Geiser for reviewing its technical accuracy, and Karen Helde for double-checking all the sites, and offering some of her own.

To the SYBEX production team of desktop publisher Thomas Goudie and proofreader/production assistant Kim Askew-Qasem, and to indexer Ted Laux, for their dedicated and timely devotion to the many tasks that go into making a quality book.

To Linda for her constant love, encouragement, and help in a pinch.

And to Isabel, who makes everything special.

Table of Contents

Introduction

The Internet, the easily accessible but ever changing, ever expanding, global computer network, is pretty much a place of benevolent chaos. There is something out there for every interest, including an interest in the law. Finding what interests you, though, is where problems arise. I've been at this for some time now, and in talking with friends, colleagues, and acquaintances, it seems to me that people interested in the Internet and what you can do or find there have at least one of the following problems.

◆ One, you're interested in the Internet but you don't know how to get there.

◆ Two, you have Internet access but you don't know how to find what you'd like to find.

◆ Three, you have Internet access and enough expertise to find what you want, but there is so much available and so much to choose from that you just don't have the time to wade through it all.

This *Pocket Tour* will help solve all these problems for you. It's a guide to using the Internet to find places ("sites") that make legal and law-related information available.

For people with the first problem mentioned above—how to get on the Internet—turn to *Part One*, which is a short primer on the Internet. You'll learn about the kinds of things you can find and do out there in cyberspace. I'll discuss how you go about getting access, and I'll cover what kinds of software you can use. There's important information about accepted behavior, or "Netiquette," and a useful glossary of Internet jargon.

For people with the second and third problems above, *Part Two* contains the sites that I think will appeal to the interests of lawyers and nonlawyers alike, sites that stand out because of the quality and/or quantity of the information they contain, or because of the design and execution of the site. I've tried to put together a broad cross-section of quality sites, but I've made no attempt to be comprehensive and include every site that has something to do with law. There are enough boring or redundant sites out there; there's no reason to put them all in a book.

Since the *Pocket Tour of Law* is modeled on a travel guide, each site has its own entry. Each entry describes what you'll find at the site, what the strengths and weaknesses of the site are, and of course what needs or interests the site might address. In addition, each entry tells you where to find the site (i.e., it gives you the address) and what kind of site it is (i.e., a page on the World Wide Web, a Gopher site, etc.).

The Internet is by definition international, but most of this book, for reasons of space and language, focuses on United States law. However, there a number of entries from Canada, and there are two sections devoted to international law and the law of other nations.

ORGANIZATION, AND KEY TO SYMBOLS

First, I fully expect that you are not going to read the book from front cover to back cover. Part One contains the basics on the Internet, so if you need to read it, please do, but if you're already an Internaut, as they say, you can safely skip to Part Two, where the sites are arranged into sections by subject. To begin with, you'll find sections dealing with different areas of the law (intellectual property, consumer law, taxes, etc.). Other sections contain federal and state government sites, a "lawyer's desk reference," sites on international law and laws of other nations, sites on law schools (for would-be lawyers, but also for teachers and current students), and more. The last section lists sites that offer powerful search tools, for when you get really serious about finding what you want on the Internet. Within each section, sites are usually arranged alphabetically by name. If I put a couple of the sections in a more useful order, I hope you don't mind. You can always check for what you're looking for in the Table of Contents or the Index.

As for conventions, you will find an assortment of icons indicating various helpful items. The first three are just different types of notes calling your attention to something, as follows:

This icon is for notes that give you additional information.

The key icon is for helpful hints.

The warning icon tells you to take extra care.

Every entry in Part Two is marked with an icon that indicates what kind of site you're looking at and therefore what kind of Internet tool you need to access it.

This marks a site on the World Wide Web. The majority of sites in the Pocket Tour are Web sites.

This marks a Gopher site. Most of the sites that aren't Web sites are Gopher sites.

This marks a Telnet site.

This marks a Usenet news group.

This marks a list mailing or e-mail list.

DISCLAIMER

Finally, because I'm a lawyer, I have to put in a disclaimer. Before you get started, you should remember that the Internet is constantly growing and constantly changing. Sites are added and deleted and sites change. Thus when you access a site, it may be different than what is described in the book, or it may have moved, or it may no longer exist. Be prepared for these surprises.

Further, I should point out that this book is not intended as legal advice and you should NOT rely upon it as such. It is for informational purposes only and represents only my personal opinions about Internet sites that concern the law. If you have a problem and need legal help, legal advice, or legal assistance of any kind, you should consult an attorney. Or, if you prefer to hear all of this in "legalese": **This publication is designed to provide, and efforts have been made to provide, accurate and authoritative information regarding its subject matter as of the date of publication. It is sold with the understanding that neither the author nor the publisher is engaged in rendering legal or other professional service. If legal advice or other expert assistance is required, the services of a competent professional person should be sought.**

I'd be happy to hear any suggestions you may have about the Pocket Tour of Law. *You can reach me by e-mail at* 74654.3441@compuserve.com.

Part One:
The Basics

What Can I Do on the Internet?

This book has two parts. The first, this one, provides a general overview of using the Internet—what types of things you'll be doing once you get onto the Internet, and, significantly, how to get onto the Internet in the first place. If you're already a seasoned Internet explorer, feel free to skip directly to Part Two, which presents the best and most popular law-related sites and resources on the Internet.

In this section of Part One, I'll set out the most useful features of the Internet, to give you a sense of what you can do over the Internet:

Send and Receive *E-mail*

Read and Post Messages to *Usenet Newsgroups*

Read and Post Messages to Subscription Newsletters ("*Lists*")

Browse the *World Wide Web*

Tunnel for Information Using *Gopher*

Log On to Remote Computers Using *Telnet*

Transfer Files with *FTP*

In later sections, I'll discuss what's available for getting onto the Internet, including the various types of Internet service providers and Internet software.

SEND AND RECEIVE E-MAIL

E-mail (electronic mail) is probably the first thing people want to try when they get on the Internet. E-mail really is amazing; it offers near-instantaneous communication with people all over the world. Even if you're not much of a letter writer, you may find yourself writing a lot of e-mail. My wife and I have regular e-mail correspondence with people on either side of the United States, and in Canada, Germany, Turkey, and Sweden. And the cost is less than you'd expect: Despite the fact that many or all of the people you may correspond with via e-mail may be spread around the country or around the world, it usually takes only a local call to connect to the Internet and then send or receive e-mail.

In addition to sending messages, an increasing number of e-mail programs let you send files as well as messages.

All of this has significant application in a business setting. Sending messages avoids extended games of "telephone tag," and sending files allows for cooperative work, even when workers are in different cities—and it's cheaper than faxing.

MAKING SENSE OF E-MAIL ADDRESSES

Sending mail of any kind, of course, requires you to know your recipient's address. As with regular mail addresses, you may have to call a person first just to ask them what their e-mail address is. E-mail addresses can, at first glance, seem odd. For one thing, it all goes on a single line. Your colleague might dictate to you something that, when written down, looks something like this:

alvin@zinnia.berkeley.edu

or something at least as impenetrable, like

74654.3441@compuserve.com

Actually, though, e-mail addresses work a lot like postal addresses. Say, for example, that you wanted to send me a letter. You could write care of the publisher at this address:

Michael Gross, author

C/O SYBEX Inc.

2021 Challenger Dr.

Alameda, CA

(We'll ignore ZIP codes in this explanation because they are actually a separate addressing system.) Now, if you had to deliver this letter yourself, how would you do it? First you'd look at the *last* line of the address and know that you'd need first of all to get to California. Once you got to California, you'd need to go to the city of Alameda. In Alameda, you'd have to find Challenger Drive; on Challenger Drive you'd have to find building 2021, and in that building, you'd have to make sure you gave the letter to someone who works for SYBEX Inc. You'd have to trust that at that point someone at SYBEX will take care of ("C/O") getting the letter to my mailbox in the company mailroom.

In short, to deliver mail, you'd read from the bottom up—you'd identify the largest or most general location in the address and then narrow your focus progressively until you got to the mailbox of the person you're writing to.

E-mail delivery works in much the same way. When you send an e-mail message, the computer delivering the message looks first to the most general location found in the e-mail address, and then looks to a more specific location within that location, and so on, until it finds the recipient's electronic mailbox located on a particular machine or a particular system.

For example, instead of having to know what state your intended recipient lives in, the most general location you need to know for an e-mail address is the *top-level domain*. Within the United States there are six top-level domains.

Domain	Meaning
.com	Commercial organization
.edu	Educational institution
.gov	Government organization (non-military)
.mil	Military institution
.net	Network service or provider
.org	Other organization (i.e., none of the above)

The top-level domain is always the rightmost segment of an e-mail address. My e-mail address, for example, puts me within a commercial organization:

74654.3441@compuserve.com

In fact, my e-mail address is an example of the basic e-mail address format. On the far right is the top-level domain: .com, for commercial organizations. To the left of the top-level domain but to the right of the "at" sign (the @ symbol) is the *domain*, or computer system on which my electronic mailbox is found: the CompuServe Information Service, represented as compuserve. To the left of the "at" sign, is my *username*, which in this case is just a number: 74654.3441.

Some addresses are more complex— as you've probably seen. Such addresses, like this one, look like our other example above:

alvin@zinnia.berkeley.edu

These more complicated addresses exist because many computer systems or domains are divided into smaller groupings called *subdomains*. This fictitious address might belong to a user named alvin whose electronic mailbox is located on a computer named zinnia (the subdomain), one of many computers on the system at the University of California at Berkeley (the domain .berkeley), which is an educational institution (.edu).

Outside the United States— The top-level domain for an address outside of the United States is not one of the six listed above. Instead, it is a two-letter country code. The addresses for my wife's colleagues in Canada end with .ca, German addresses end with .de (Deutschland), and a good friend of ours would consider her life much enriched if she would just get an e-mail message from someone in Vanuatu, .vu.

READ AND POST MESSAGES TO USENET NEWSGROUPS

Another extremely popular feature of the Internet is the *Usenet newsgroups*. These are the electronic equivalents of community bulletin boards, where anyone who wishes may *post* an e-mail message, often called in this context an "article," and anyone else can read it, and respond to it if they wish.

In order to avoid what would otherwise be an unmanageable crush of articles if there were only one place to post them—a bulletin board of babel, you might say—there are upwards of 8,000 different newsgroups, with more created all the time. Each group is devoted to a single topic, so it's a fair assumption that at least one will appeal to your interest and taste. For example, the newsgroup misc.taxes is a forum for discussing and asking questions about your taxes, and misc.legal is a wide-ranging discussion of legal issues and questions. Figure 1.1 shows the subjects of a selection of articles recently posted there.

- Re: DOES CA have a FOIA? - Michael Stone (12)
- Tax Court: Hubbard Made Money From CoS. [2 of 2] - Name withheld by request (329)
- for the cause - Prince/Darkness (36)
- Court: Hubbard Made Money From Church of Scientology - Q Mixmaster Remailer (370)
- Capital Punishment Info? - Fenner (7)
- Re: Petition for National Service - Arnold Williams (33)
- UL's from The Guardian's weekend page - snopes (33)
- Re: TELEMARKETING Stop it NOW (repost) - Mark Phaedrus (21)
- Re: CALL FOR SUBMISSIONS: Homolka/Teale/Bernardo FAQ v4.1 - Chris Lewis (78)
- Re: Why software patents cannot work - Stan Friesen (28)
- LAST WORD: Definition of "tele-" - Jasper O'Malley (23)
- Re: Need an AABBS Update!!! - Robert Reed (7)
- K Mart Canada Limited fined $200,000 for misleading advertising - Nigel Allen (55)
- PRESS RELEASE - FACTnet online again - Name withheld by request (66)
- Did Mullis Invent PCR All By Himself -- Or Was It A Group Effort? - merlin (36)

Figure 1.1:
A selection of articles recently posted to the misc.legal newsgroup

You can find a list of current newsgroups posted periodically in the following newsgroups: news.lists, news.groups, news.announce.newusers, news.answers, *and* news.newsites. *You might find, though, that because some Internet providers only give access to a limited (though still quite large) selection of Usenet newsgroups, some of the groups listed are unavailable to you.*

UNDERSTANDING NEWSGROUP NAMES

As you may have gathered from the few groups mentioned above, the name of a newsgroup describes its subject. Newsgroups are divided into eight large categories, which appear as the first segment in a newsgroup's name.

Category	Meaning
alt.	Alternative topics
comp.	Computers and computer science

Category	Meaning
misc.	Miscellaneous or general discussions
news.	Discussions about newsgroups themselves as a topic
rec.	Recreation
sci.	Sciences
soc.	Social concerns
talk.	"Soapbox debates," sort of the electronic equivalent of talk radio

These most-general categories can be further divided into subcategories, and further divided into sub-subcategories as you read from left to right in a newsgroup's name. (Unlike an e-mail address, a newsgroup name narrows in focus as you read from left to right.) For example, one group I mentioned above, misc.legal, contains articles concerning miscellaneous general legal issues; misc.legal.moderated, which is also a general legal discussion, contains articles that must first pass the inspection of a person known as the moderator, who deletes articles that are deemed irrelevant or redundant.

READ AND POST MESSAGES TO SUBSCRIPTION NEWSLETTERS ("LISTS")

Lists, or, more precisely, *list mailings*, are something of a cross between e-mail and newsgroups—they are messages and articles sent out to people who have asked to receive those messages and articles. In other words, they are the e-mail equivalents of subscription newsletters.

Like newsgroups, there are large numbers of lists, each devoted to discussing a particular topic. Unlike newsgroups, however, list mailings are sent directly to the electronic mailboxes of subscribers.

 If you decide to participate in lists, plan to to check your e-mail at least once a day. If you let it go for even a few days, you may very well come back to a few hundred messages.

Any person who wishes to participate in a list can read and respond to its messages. All you have to do to participate in a list is *subscribe*, which means sending a short, specific message to a given e-mail address. The message and e-mail address are different for each list. For example, to subscribe to the list cpscinfo-l, run by the Consumer Products Safety Commission, and on which are posted CPSC product-recall and product-safety announcements, you must send the message

sub CPSCINFO-L yourfirstname yourlastname

to listproc@cpsc.gov. Unsubscribing or ending your participation in a list is accomplished with a similar instruction. The exact subscription and cancellation commands differ for each list. Cpscinfo-l and other law-related *lists* are discussed in greater detail in Part Two.

Warning: Every message you (or others) send to a list is automatically delivered to the mailbox of every person on the list.

BROWSE THE WORLD WIDE WEB

The *World Wide Web* (also called "WWW" or simply "the Web") is currently the most popular and fastest growing part of the Internet, and justly so. The first reason for the Web's popularity is presentation. The Web combines text and *graphics*, and sometimes even animation and sound, on a computerized "page." Figure 1.2 shows a Web page concerning the Supreme Court of Canada. You can see the logo of the organization that brings you the page, a picture of the Court itself, and below this, some introductory information.

Figure 1.2:
The Supreme Court of Canada on the World Wide Web

Often in Web parlance you will hear the term home page. *A home page is no different than any other Web page, really. The term usually refers to the first page you see when you connect to a site or location on the Web. A site will generally use its home page to identify itself and to provide an overview of what is available to you there.*

Now take a look at the text on the top page of Figure 1.3, a home page for DIANA, An International Human Rights Database, located on a server at

DIANA

An International Human Rights Database

Dedicated to completing the pioneering work in human rights information of <u>Diana Vincent-Daviss</u>

The DIANA project is grateful for the generous support of the Ohio Board of Regents, the National Center for Automated Information Research and the United States Institute for Peace.

<u>Primary Human Rights Sources</u>

<u>Secondary Human Rights Sources</u>

Press <u>here</u> for a link to the Law School Constitutional Repository at the University of the Witwatersrand, Johannesburg, South Africa. Among the materials of interest at this site are the opinions in the recent death penalty case.

DIANA is an on-line resource inspired by the life and work of Professor Diana Vincent-Daviss, the late Deputy Director of the Orville H. Schell, Jr. Center for International Human Rights and librarian of Yale Law School. Professor Vincent-Daviss was a comprehensive bibliographer of literature on human rights. This service is named DIANA in her honor. DIANA has been established by the Schell Center, the Urban Morgan Institute for Human Rights, the Center for Electronic Text in the Law, the Yale Law Library and the University of Cincinnati College of Law Library. DIANA is designed to promote the creation,

Figure 1.3:
Top: The home page for DIANA, An International Human Rights Database. This page is located at a server in Cincinnati. By clicking on a link, you automatically get to...
Bottom: The home page of the Law School Constitutional Repository, University of the Witwatersrand, Johannesburg, South Africa.

 # Welcome to WITS <u>Law School</u>

Welcome to the Law School Constitutional Repository, University of the Witwatersrand, Johannesburg, South Africa.

Please read our <u>disclaimer</u>.

What we have available at our site:

- South African Constitutional Court <u>Opinions</u>
- Constitutional <u>Documents</u>
- <u>About</u> the Court and the Judges
- Links to other sites of <u>legal interest</u>

Other sites:

- WWW at <u>SUNSITE</u>, WITS
- WWW Servers available in <u>South Africa</u>
- Other WWW Servers in the <u>World</u>

the University of Cinncinnati. You'll see that parts of the text are underlined. (If your eyes are really good, you might be able to see that the underlined text is also a different shade of gray than the text adjacent to it. On screen this underlined text is a different color.) These pieces of underlined text are the second reason the Web is so exciting. These are *hyperlinks*, more often called just *links*. All pages on the Web are interconnected by means of these links. If you use your mouse to point to a link and click, you are automatically taken to a different, but related, page. This is not to say that every Web page is linked to every other Web page. Rather, every page is linked to a number of others, which are linked to still others, and so forth.

Halfway down the page shown in the top of Figure 1.3, one of the paragraphs begins with "Press here for a link...." When I clicked on the link I was automatically connected—across an ocean and into the southern hemisphere—to the second page displayed in Figure 1.3.

So you see, clicking on a link can take you to a related page on a completely different computer system, which could be anywhere on the Internet. It could be in the next city, the next state, or on a different continent entirely.

The Web is now so rich and offers so much, people I know have spent entire afternoons browsing around, following links, and seeing the sites.

URLS: HOW TO READ WEB "ADDRESSES"

What with all their links to other Web pages, it would be impossible to fit most Web pages into single categories. Which raises the question of how you go about finding things. There is, after all, no real beginning or end to the Web. One very common approach to finding things on it is having someone you know tell you where to find a page, by giving you its address. Addresses, in Web parlance, are called *URLs*, or *Uniform Resource Locators*.

 There are also powerful search programs available on the Web to help you get to where you want to go. Many are identified for you at the end of Part Two.

Every page has a unique URL. URLs are somewhat longer and somewhat uglier than e-mail addresses, but really aren't any more difficult to understand. The URL of the Supreme Court of Canada page in Figure 1.2 is:

http://www.droit.umontreal.ca/CSC.html

There are three parts to this address, each separated by slashes. The first part of the URL, http://, designates the *protocol*, or system for exchanging information, that computers on the Web use. While other protocols can and do exist, HTTP, which stands for *Hypertext Transfer Protocol*, is the de facto standard on the Web. Every URL you are likely to see will begin with http://.

Skipping to the last part of the URL, in this case CSC.html, you find *the name of the file* containing the information displayed on the page. The filename suffix .html stands for *Hypertext Markup Language*. It is the standard Web-page file type.

The middle part of the URL, the part between the slashes, you might recognize from the earlier discussion of e-mail addresses. This is the complete *domain and subdomain address* of the computer system on which the page file is located.

As with e-mail addresses, more complicated URLs abound. For example, you may see URLs that include the complete *path name* as part of the Web page's .html file name, in which case there will be additional slashes, as in this URL for another Web page from the Supreme Court of Canada:

http://www.droit.umontreal.ca/opengov/s-court/sc.home.html

In this case, sc.home.html is the page's file name, and the information directly preceding it, /opengov/s-court/, identifies the directory path to that file on the Web site's computer.

You may find still other types of URLs that include additional types of information, such as "port numbers," to help your Web browser locate the files it needs on the various types of computers that make information available over the Web.

TUNNEL FOR INFORMATION USING GOPHER

Gopher is a somewhat older and certainly less glamorous Internet feature than the World Wide Web. It gets its name because it was created at the University of Minnesota, whose mascot is the Golden Gopher. In tech-talk, Gopher is a distributed document delivery system. In English, Gopher provides a uniform way to retrieve information from the Internet. As you can see in Figure 1.4, Gopher structures information as a menu.

Pictured in Figure 1.4 is a Gopher provided by the United States Library of Congress to display information about the United States Copyright office. Items marked with a document icon are information files that you can read. Items marked with a folder are submenus of the current menu; select one of these to have Gopher take you to a list of additional items to choose from. Every Gopher site you see is structured in this hierarchical way.

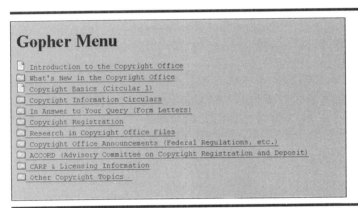

Gopher Menu

- Introduction to the Copyright Office
- What's New in the Copyright Office
- Copyright Basics (Circular 1)
- Copyright Information Circulars
- In Answer to Your Query (Form Letters)
- Copyright Registration
- Research in Copyright Office Files
- Copyright Office Announcements (Federal Regulations, etc.)
- ACCORD (Advisory Committee on Copyright Registration and Deposit)
- CARP & Licensing Information
- Other Copyright Topics

Figure 1.4:
A Gopher menu from the United States Library of Congress. This one is displaying copyright information.

ADVANTAGES AND DISADVANTAGES OF GOPHER

One obvious disadvantage that Gopher has when compared to the Web is its looks. With Gopher you get text, text, and more text, and no beautiful graphical pages. Within this disadvantage, however, lurks an advantage. Web pages, particularly ones that contain many graphics, are quite large—that is, the files are large—and it can take a while to transmit all of that data to your machine. In short, the Web can be *slow*. Gopher, plain though it may be, is comparatively fast and efficient. You don't have to wait around for large quantities of data to reach you; text travels quickly when it's alone.

In addition, Gopher is ubiquitous; you'll find huge amounts of information accessible through Gopher all over the Internet, and it's easy to use. You just march up and down a hierarchical menu structure.

 As with the Web, finding information on Gopher can be difficult since there is so much of it. Fortunately, as with the Web, there are Gopher search programs that allow you to search "Gopherspace." These are called, in what I can only imagine to be programmer humor, Archie, Veronica, and Jughead.

HOW TO READ GOPHER ADDRESSES

Finally, like the Web and e-mail, Gopher sites have addresses. These however, are quite simple, being nothing other than the subdomain and domain address of the computer system on which the Gopher is located. The address for the Library of Congress Gopher shown in Figure 1.4 is marvel.loc.gov.

LOG ON TO REMOTE COMPUTERS USING TELNET

 Telnet is a different tool than either Gopher or the World Wide Web. If you've ever gone into a library and used one of its card catalog computers, you've used what is called a *dumb terminal*. These poor machines are so named because, although they provide a monitor and a keyboard to connect you to the library's computerized card catalog, the computer itself is located elsewhere in the building, or might even be in another building or on another campus. Telnet temporarily turns your desktop computer into a dumb terminal so that you can access a remote computer and use it as if you were sitting at a terminal connected directly to it. Telnet is, then, yet another way of making Internet information available to the public.

Libraries frequently provide Telnet access to their catalogs. Figure 1.5, for example, shows the main menu of the Columbia University Law Library catalog and Figure 1.6 shows the results of a search of the same catalog for a leading treatise on the law of evidence. At the time I logged into this catalog, I was at home in California and nowhere near New York City.

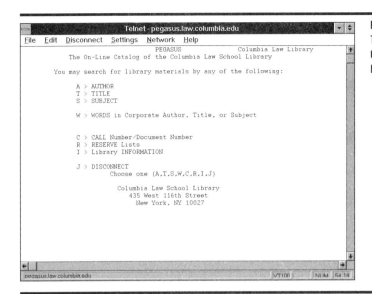

Figure 1.5:
The main menu of the
Columbia University
Law Library Catalog

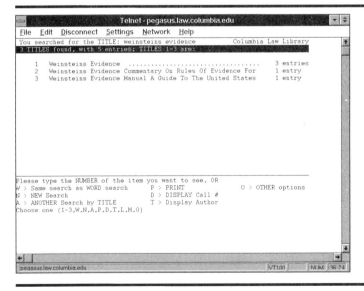

Figure 1.6:
The results of a search
for a leading treatise
on Evidence by Federal
District Court Judge
Jack Weinstein

Telnet is useful for more than scanning the collections of libraries. You can, for example, search an index of registered copyrights at the Library of Congress; this can be found at the address loc.locis.gov.

NAVIGATING WITH TELNET

Unlike Gopher, Telnet does not provide a uniform interface between you and the information you are looking at. In fact, Telnet doesn't provide an interface at all. Since it makes your machine act as a dumb terminal, you'll see whatever interface is presented by the system you log in to. While there can be some variety, you'll often find some kind of hierarchical menu structure. Sometimes help is available and sometimes it's not, which isn't exactly reassuring. In most cases, however, the initial screen or main menu identifies the commands to use for starting over or quitting. It's a good idea to take note of these commands, because it's easy to get in over your head with Telnet. Of course, if all else fails, you can just quit your Telnet program to escape from the Telnet session.

READING TELNET ADDRESSES

The addresses of Telnet sites follow the same rules as addresses for e-mail and Gopher (refer to the discussion "Making Sense of E-mail Addresses" earlier in this part). Telnet addresses are the subdomain and domain address of the computer system to which you connect. The address for the Columbia University Law Library, for example, is

pegasus.law.columbia.edu

as seen in Figures 1.5 and 1.6.

TRANSFER FILES WITH FTP

FTP, or *File Transfer Protocol*, is a standard scheme for exchanging files among Internet computers of every stripe. It doesn't matter if you're using a PC or a Mac or a workstation or a mainframe; if you find an FTP site you can copy files from it. There are many collections of files or archives out there accessible by FTP. There is, for example, an archive of federal tax forms available at fwux.fedworld.gov.

ANONYMOUS VERSUS RESTRICTED FTP

Occasionally you will hear people refer to *anonymous FTP*. This name comes about from the way you access a public FTP site. When logging on to a public FTP site, you must give your user name or login name as "anonymous" and your complete e-mail address as a password. If you give any name other than anonymous, you can't get in.

If the FTP site you reach isn't the anonymous sort, access is restricted to people with an authorized user name and password.

READING FTP ADDRESSES

FTP addresses are no different than Telnet or Gopher addresses—just the subdomain and domain address of the system on which the FTP site is located. (Refer to the discussion "Making Sense of E-mail Addresses" earlier in this part.)

Getting on the Internet

A few years ago, before the Internet became as universal as lawyer jokes, getting connected was the hardest part of using the Internet. In those days, if you weren't an academic or connected to a research institution, access was very hard to get. Today, a large and growing number of commercial enterprises offer a wide range of Internet services.

Even today, though, if you're affiliated with a college, university, or scientific establishment (or a growing number of businesses), the at-work or at-school accounts are among the best you can get—because if your school or employer is connected to the Internet, you can probably get an account at the ideal price. Namely, *free*.

Naturally, some free accounts have limitations. For example, you may be able to read Usenet newsgroups but not post to them. Even given these limitations, a free account may very well do everything you want.

Commercial accounts range from the large *multiple-service providers* to *Internet-only providers*, which provide little more than a pathway and no special guidance.

 Whatever kind of service you use to access the Internet, if you expect to browse the World Wide Web you should have at least a 9600bps modem. Anything less than that is excruciatingly slow.

GETTING CONNECTED VIA MULTIPLE-SERVICE PROVIDERS

Because so many people now access the Internet through providers of multiple services, I'll begin by describing what you get when you use these services. Multiple-service providers not only give you a link to the Internet, they provide forums, news, weather, games, and reference materials that are exclusive to that service. The best known of these multiple-service providers are America Online, CompuServe, and Prodigy. (To be sure, there are also other, smaller services out there, but these are the most popular, and are available nation-wide.) I'll discuss each of these briefly, in alphabetical order.

VIA AMERICA ONLINE (AOL)

America Online (AOL) has experienced the fastest growth of any multiple-service provider over the last two years. AOL has the usual reference sections, news, weather, and technical support bulletin boards for all sorts of software and hardware topics. More than any other service, they offer live real-time "chat" groups and often host discussions/interviews with the famous and infamous alike.

AOL offers very easy access to all the popular features of the Internet. Everything is done with a simple point-and-click and every window has help available. Even mailing lists and Gophers are simple to use because AOL's graphical interface is simple and well thought out.

AOL Pluses: AOL is rapidly adding access at 28.8kbps. If you have a 28.8kbps modem, this is an excellent way of communicating on the Internet. Everything will move much more quickly—especially since AOL's 28.8kbps connections appear to be remarkably solid (your modem will rarely have to fall back to a slower rate because of bad connections).

VIA COMPUSERVE

CompuServe Information Service (CompuServe or CIS for short) is the granddaddy of the online world, having reached the ripe old age (in computer terms) of ten years plus. As befits any multiple-service provider, CompuServe offers news, weather, reference databases, and hundreds of special-interest forums.

CompuServe is the only one of the big three that doesn't require the use of proprietary software. You can use their Windows, Macintosh, or DOS software, or you can use any of a half-dozen programs designed for it by other developers. To access the Internet via a CompuServe account, you can use any software that can utilize a PPP connection.

For Windows users, the easiest method is to use the Windows CompuServe Information Manager (WinCIM). WinCIM enables you to use most of the Internet services, including FTP, Telnet, and newsgroups. The interface is uncluttered and easy to use, and WinCIM's newsgroup reader is one of the best.

Macintosh and OS/2 versions of the CompuServe Information Manager are available from CompuServe for no additional charge. Both systems can easily use the Internet services provided by CIS.

If you want to use the World Wide Web through CompuServe, you'll need a Web browser. CompuServe provides a version of Mosaic that can be downloaded from the CompuServe network. (Use the GO NETLAUNCHER command.)

CompuServe Pluses: The CIS connection to the Internet is as good as or better than most. In addition to good Internet access, CIS is unequaled in its forums and databases—particularly in the area of software and hardware support. Furthermore, CompuServe is in the process of adding more 28.8kbps connection points, and plans to have several hundred in operation by the end of the year.

VIA PRODIGY

Prodigy was the first of the multiple-service providers to become known, through advertising in the mainstream media, to the general public. It offers news, weather, investment information, special-interest discussion groups, and services aimed particularly at families.

Although Prodigy was one of the last of the popular multiple-service providers to offer e-mail, on the other hand, it was the first to offer any access to the Internet *beyond* e-mail. In late 1994, they introduced their own proprietary World Wide Web browser.

With the Web connection made, it was but a small step for Prodigy to add newsgroups and Gopher and FTP capability. All of these can be used by any Prodigy member who has sufficient hardware and software.

Macintosh users currently have access only to Internet mail and newsgroups. Prodigy plans to add WWW, FTP, and Gopher access for Macintoshes by the end of 1995.

Prodigy Minuses: Outside of the Internet features, Prodigy is awash with advertising. Every screen has an ad of some kind. All those graphics slow your access, and even a 14.4kbps connection on Prodigy feels slower than on other services.

GETTING CONNECTED VIA INTERNET-ONLY PROVIDERS

Overall, America Online, CompuServe, and Prodigy are not for the heavy user of the Internet. If that turns out to describe you, you'll probably be better off turning to an Internet-only provider, a commercial service whose sole business is providing access to the Internet.

The main disadvantage, of course, of going with such a service is that you don't get all of the other, non-Internet features offered by the large providers. No forums, no file libraries, no chat rooms, etc. Just the Internet.

The advantage of using Internet-only providers is that all they do is Internet, so to speak, and they do it well. Another possible advantage is cost. If you spend a lot of time on the Internet and your multiple-service provider charges by the hour, you will quickly spend quite a bit of money. Many Internet-only providers, by contrast, charge a flat, monthly fee, usually in the $25-to-$40 a month range for about that many hours of connect-time, more than enough time for just about anyone. The longer you are connected to a flat rate service, then, the smaller your actual cost per hour gets. See the "Costs and Money Matters" section later in this part for a more complete discussion of other factors that influence your out-of-pocket Internet costs.

WHAT YOU WILL GET

An account with an Internet-only provider is likely to be a special kind of account called a *SLIP account* or a *PPP account*. At a highly technical level, well beyond the scope of this book, there are differences between SLIP and PPP. For our purposes, though, they are functionally identical; it doesn't matter whether you get one or the other. SLIP stands for *Serial Line Internet Protocol* and PPP stands for *Point to Point Protocol*. What these protocols—these accounts—do is allow you to connect a computer directly to the Internet over a modem and a telephone line. When you connect to the Internet through a SLIP or PPP account, your machine becomes an actual part of the Internet for the duration of your call.

 SLIP and PPP accounts are good economical ways to get yourself connected to the Internet.

In order to use your SLIP or PPP account, your provider will also set you up with special communication software that you must use to call in and connect to your account. Because data is sent between Internet computers according to a particular protocol, you can't use an ordinary, general-purpose telecommunications program such as Procomm Plus for this. In addition to the software needed to access your SLIP or PPP account, your Internet-only provider may also provide you with the software needed to go cruising on the Net.

NETCOM'S NETCRUISER ACCOUNT

NetCom communications offers an attractive Internet-only account called a NetCruiser account. The account is named for NetCruiser, NetCom's Windows-based Internet program, which NetCom provides to you with your account. (Figure 1.7). NetCruiser is an all-in-one package that will dial your modem to connect you to your account *and* provide easy access to all Internet tools. It has a mail program, a news reader (a program used to read and post newsgroup articles), a World Wide Web browser, Gopher, Telnet, and FTP programs. It even has a few Internet programs not discussed here (I don't discuss them because they aren't really useful in pursuing law information on the Internet).

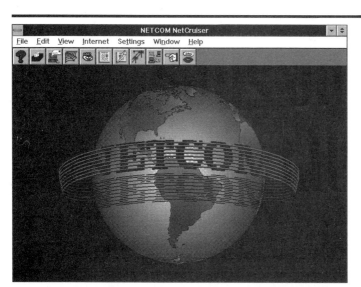

Figure 1.7:
The main screen of NetCom's NetCruiser. The buttons across the top start NetCruiser's Internet tools. Notice the Gopher button and the button with the Web on it.

NetCom is, so far, the only Internet-only provider with a nationwide presence. By the time you read this, there may be more.

NetCom provides local telephone access in most major metropolitan areas.

OTHER INTERNET-ONLY PROVIDERS

NetCom is by no means the only SLIP/PPP provider out there, although it has the advantage of a nationwide presence. If you are more comfortable with a smaller, local provider that perhaps will provide better service, it is not difficult to find one.

If you know someone who has an e-mail account, or perhaps you have access to one yourself, you can easily get a large listing of Internet providers called Pdial. To get Pdial, send an e-mail message with no subject, that says only:

send pdial to type.your.complete.e-mail.address.here

and Pdial will automatically be sent to your e-mailbox.

Pdial is also available from the Electronic Frontier Foundation's FTP archive. The address is ftp.eff.org. *The pdial file name is* pdial015.list *and it is found in the* /pub/Net_info/Resources *directory. While you are there, you will find a similar list in a file called* us_providers_internic.list.

Alternatively, you can browse the classified ads in your local computer publications, or check out that monster of a computer magazine called *Computer Shopper.*

Finally, there is no better way to find a good provider than word of mouth. Check with friends or colleagues who are into the Internet; they are the best resource.

COST AND MONEY MATTERS

Unless your Internet account is free or offers unlimited access for a flat fee, there are a number of factors that go into how much the Internet will cost you—factors that go beyond how much you pay per hour or how many free hours you get.

Choosing a Local Phone Number: It's particularly important to choose carefully the phone number you'll use to connect to your provider. Free access can turn out to be far from free if you're paying ten cents a minute (or more) in local toll charges.

Joining a service that has a connecting phone number that is a true local call (not a toll call) is ideal. If you find such a connection, make sure that your phone service is set up for free unlimited local calls (not measured message rate—that'll add up at a furious rate).

If you have to use a toll connection, look around for the connection point or access number that's closest. Consider, though, that if you live near a state line, a call to a neighboring state can paradoxically be less per minute than an intrastate call.

Choosing Access Times: Some services have very different rates depending on when you use the system. For example, a service may charge a high hourly rate during the day and give you unlimited free access in so-called off hours such as nights and weekends.

On the other hand, if you're paying by the minute no matter when you sign on, you'll save money if you use the system when it's less busy. Time on the system is allocated in time slices: as the system gets busier the slices get smaller and smaller. In effect, the busier the line, the more your computer is spending time waiting in line than it is sending and receiving information.

Almost all systems are busier in the evenings. When you have files to download, you can often get a faster transmission rate if you schedule your session when the majority of the country is in bed: early in the morning (eastern U.S.) or late at night (western U.S.). Of course, if you're FTPing to a computer in Japan or Switzerland, it's difficult to figure out a "good" time, you may as well just do it when it's a good time for you.

Internet Software for Internet-Only Accounts

While NetCom's NetCruiser, which is discussed above, will only work with a NetCom account, there is plenty of outstanding Internet software available should you decide on a different Internet-only provider. In this section I'll present a few of the most popular Internet software packages, some of which may come with your Internet-only account. If they do, so much the better for you. Indeed, before you sign up for an Internet-only account, you should find out what software you get with it. If the answer is nothing, or you later discover that you don't really like the Web browser or mail program you did get, you might want to consider switching to one of the following programs.

NETSCAPE AND MOSAIC

Two World Wide Web browsers, *Netscape* and *Mosaic*, are the absolute cream of the crop. Browsers are the programs that allow you to see the Web in all of its glory. Mosaic, created at the National Center for Supercomputing Applications (NCSA) at the University of Illinois, Champaign-Urbana, is the original. Netscape, from Netscape Communications Corp., is the current market leader. Both of these programs are extremely well thought out and well executed. They allow you to take full advantage, not only of the World Wide Web, but other parts of the Internet as well.

 Although there are a number of "flavors" of Mosaic on the market now, from different manufacturers, each version that has the word Mosaic in its name is essentially Mosaic.

First, of course, Mosaic and Netscape can display the text and graphics on Web pages clearly and crisply. Figure 1.8 shows THOMAS, a Web page from Congress with a good deal of legislative information, including the full text of the Congressional Record and of all laws passed since the 103rd Congress, as displayed by Mosaic.

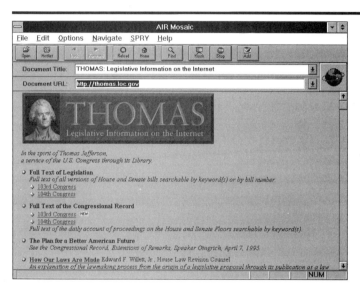

Figure 1.8:
THOMAS shown in
Mosaic

As I mentioned earlier, graphics, especially those found on many Web pages, can slow things down for you; it can take a long time for all of the data that makes up the graphics to be sent to your computer. Netscape and some of the Mosaics, therefore, allow you to view Web pages with the pictures turned off, so that the page, which is now text-only, transmits quickly. If you then decide you want to see the complete page, you can load the pictures manually. Figure 1.9 shows THOMAS in Netscape with graphics turned off.

Mosaic and Netscape are not limited to browsing the Web, however; you can also use them to browse Gopher sites, get files from FTP archives, and read and post newsgroup articles. Figure 1.10 shows Mosaic browsing the U.S. Senate's Gopher site. Figure 1.11 shows a list of articles from the newsgroup **misc.legal**, displayed in Netscape.

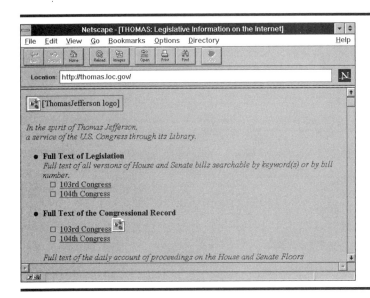

Figure 1.9:
Netscape displaying
THOMAS with pictures
turned off

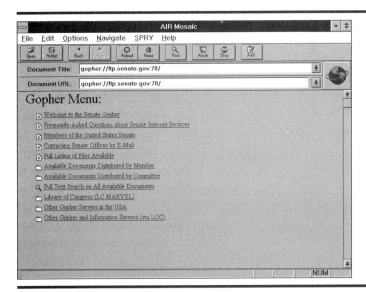

Figure 1.10:
Mosaic browsing the
U.S. Senate Gopher site

Notice the URL near the top of Figure 1.10. Since this a Gopher, the usual Web page protocol http:// is replaced by gopher://, followed by the Gopher site address. You access an FTP archive the same way, via ftp://address.

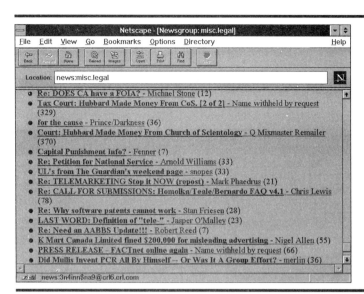

Figure 1.11:
Netscape displaying
articles from the
misc.legal newsgroup

WHERE TO GET NETSCAPE AND MOSAIC

Netscape and the original Mosaic, NCSA Mosaic, are both available on the Internet. You can download Netscape from Netscape Communications' FTP site at:

ftp.mcom.com

in the **/netscape/windows** directory.

And you can get NCSA Mosaic from NCSA at:

ftp.ncsa.uiuc.edu

in the **/Mosaic/Windows** directory.

Netscape and NCSA Mosaics are also available in Macintosh and Unix versions in the appropriately named directories at these sites.

Netscape is free for students, faculty and staff (K through college), for employees of nonprofit organizations, and for evaluation purposes. Otherwise, it costs $39 as of this writing.

NCSA Mosaic is available at no cost for academic, research, and internal business purposes.

EUDORA

Just about any Internet software you're going to come across will handle e-mail, but not all of them handle it well. If you're comfortable with the program you have, then you should probably stick with it. If, however, you can see limitations in it or you somehow seem to generate a large volume of e-mail, you might want to consider switching to Eudora.

Eudora is a *POPmail* program. This means, simply, that it allows you to take care of most of your e-mail work—reading and writing messages—when you're offline. You go online only long enough to collect any incoming messages you might have or send any messages you've composed. If you are paying for Internet service by the hour, this is a real money saver. Figure 1.12 shows Eudora and a bunch of messages recently received.

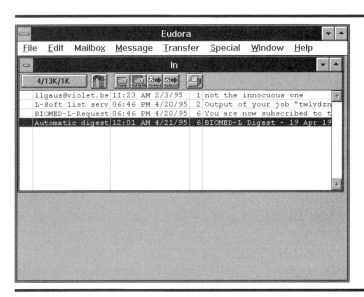

Figure 1.12:
Incoming messages
gathered by Eudora

WHERE TO GET EUDORA

Eudora is available on the Internet at

ftp.qualcomm.com

in the **/quest/eudora/windows/1.4** directory. The version available here does not cost anything, but it is "postcardware." If you use it and you like it, the author of the program has asked people to send him a postcard. A version with more advanced features is available commercially.

Netiquette

The Internet is a community that prides itself on openness and the free exchange of ideas and information. However, with the recent, explosive growth in the number of users in the last few years has come some strain. As in any community, good behavior is both appreciated and reciprocated, and bad behavior is frowned upon. With this in mind, I offer some helpful hints on Internet etiquette, or *Netiquette* for short.

IN WRITTEN COMMUNICATIONS GENERALLY

When you are speaking with someone face to face, you convey your meaning not only with the words that come out of your mouth, but also by your tone, gesture, and facial expression. When you're writing to someone, whether it be via the postal mail or via the Internet, this nonverbal component is missing. For this reason, humor and sarcasm travel badly; misunderstandings can and will occur because you wrote something you intended to be funny and it was taken as an insult.

In order to avoid this, many Internet users mark their humor and sarcasm with **<grin>** (or **<g>**) and **<smile>**. Sometimes you'll see a "smiley," also called an *emoticon*, to the same end: :=). If this just looks like punctuation mark hash to you, look at it while tilting your head to the left. I haven't even attempted to list the most interesting emoticons here, because there are so many of them. There are enough of them out there to fill an entire book.

One other convention to keep in mind when you are writing on the Internet: DON'T WRITE IN ALL CAPITAL LETTERS. When you do so, it will be assumed that you are SHOUTING and, therefore, being a bit rude.

SOME NEWSGROUP DO'S AND DON'TS

In addition to keeping in mind the above-mentioned writing conventions, here are a few things to keep in mind especially if you are going to participate in newsgroups.

◆ Before you post to a group, make sure you have a sense not only of the general subject matter but also of what has been said recently. "Lurk" for a while to get a sense of the lay of the land. As a good friend of mine puts it, "read before you write." This will keep you from posting repetitive and uninformed messages.

◆ In a similar vein, read the *FAQs* (*Frequently Asked Questions*) that explain the basics of each group. These are posted regularly in each group, usually once every two weeks or so. Also, if the group you're interested in is moderated, i.e., monitored for content, the group will have a set of written guidelines. Read these as well.

◆ The Internet is a big place, but don't get the idea that you're no more than a face in the crowd. Consider carefully what you write. Imagine the effect your criticisms or sarcasm or insults or off-color comments might have if they showed up in the mailboxes of your friends or neighbors (or even your boss) via the magic of uncontrolled copying and forwarding.

◆ Do not post advertisements. Some Internet groups allow them, but the vast majority do not and view advertisements as rude, intrusive, and a basic violation of Internet norms. You will receive many messages if you post an ad where it's not welcome—but none of them will be pleasant. So be sure to read the group's FAQ to see what the rules are.

◆ Do not "cross-post," that is, post the same message to different groups that are on similar topics. Chances are the same people read clusters of related groups and thus will see your message over and over.

◆ Finally, make judicious use of private e-mail. If all you want to do is thank someone, for example, don't post a message to the newsgroup if all it says is "thanks!" Send it by private e-mail so as not to clutter the newsgroup.

People have written entire volumes on Netiquette. If you are interested in reading further, you can find a lot more information on the Gopher of the Electronic Frontier Foundation, at gopher.eff.org, *in the* /Net_info/Net_Culture *directory.*

WHEN TRANSFERRING FILES FROM FTP SITES

FTP archives have a lot of great stuff in them. Since the archives are open to the public, it's not surprising that FTP sites have to cope with great demand. However, the demand at some sites has been so great as to disturb users who regularly work on the system that hosts the site. When this has happened, the hosts have sometimes eliminated public access entirely or sharply curtailed its hours of availability. In order to avoid such disturbance, try to confine your use of FTP until after 6pm local time for the site.

ASKING LEGAL QUESTIONS OF ATTORNEYS ON LINE

Finally, if you post a question seeking legal advice to a newsgroup, chances are attorneys will answer, but they may do so in a way you consider unsatisfactory. The answer may be in more general terms than you'd hoped, it will certainly be accompanied by a disclaimer, and possibly also be accompanied by a recommendation that you see an attorney privately. Let me try to offer an explanation.

First, it's difficult to give an answer that covers all the possibilities without knowing all of the facts that are, as we put it, legally significant. And almost every summary of a situation will be missing some legally significant facts.

Second, there is the issue of malpractice. I know when I say this that eyes roll into the backs of heads. I know that it wouldn't even occur to most people who post legal queries to a newsgroup (a) to go out and act on the advice given and then (b) turn around and sue the attorney when things don't go well. I know all of this, but the threat of such malpractice suits is still very real.

Third and finally, there is the reality of malpractice insurance. Some insurers will not cover malpractice liability arising from casual legal advice given in a forum such as this.

I hope that this sheds a little light on why some answers are given as they are.

Internet Jargon

For your reference, here is a list of common Internet terms you're likely to encounter in your cyberspace travels.

archive—A site containing a collection of files.

article—A message posted to a newsgroup.

browser—A program such as Netscape or Mosaic used to navigate the World Wide Web.

client—Software that allows you to extract some service from a server somewhere on the network. Also, the computer using such software.

domain—A collection of computers or computer systems comprising an unique location on the Internet.

FAQ—Frequently Asked Questions. Questions and answers that provide basic information for new users.

flame—A loud and boisterous personal attack. Usually provoked.

home page—The first page you see when you connect to a site on the World Wide Web.

html—Hypertext Markup Language. The coding scheme used to create World Wide Web pages. Also refers to the file format of Web pages.

host—A multi-user computer that serves as a central processor for a number of terminals. This usually means the computer that's "in charge" in a data communication network.

http—Hypertext Transfer Protocol. The standard system for exchanging information among computers on the World Wide Web. Http makes possible the hyperlinks that take you from page to page.

link or **hyperlink**—A feature of a Web page that takes you directly to another, related Web page. Links usually appear as underlined text, but can also be buttons or picture.

list server—A computer that automatically sends out mailings via e-mail to everyone on a list.

newbie—A new Internet user.

page—A single collection of text, graphics, and sometimes sound and animation on the World Wide Web; the electronic analogue to a page in a printed book.

PPP—Point to Point Protocol. Accounts using this protocol allow you to connect to the Internet over a modem.

protocol—Any standard means of exchanging data between computers.

remote login—Connecting to a computer that's not connected to you directly using local wiring. (Every computer you reach by modem is remote.)

server—Central computer in a network that processes and regulates data on the network.

site—A location on the Internet.

SLIP—Serial Line Internet Protocol. Accounts using this protocol allow you to connect directly to the Internet over a modem.

Abbreviations on the Internet

In writing things on line, you may often want to abbreviate to speed yourself through the typing. Even if you never abbreviate yourself, you're sure to run into abbreviations used by someone else. Sometimes you can get their meaning from context, but other times they're just cryptic. Here, then, are some common ones you'll find on the Internet.

BBS	Bulletin Board System
BTW	By the way
FWIW	For what it's worth
IANAL	I am not a lawyer
IMCO	In my considered opinion
IMHO	In my humble opinion
IMVHO	In my very humble opinion (usually not meant humbly)
IOW	In other words
LOL	Laughing out loud
OTOH	On the one hand/on the other hand
ROTFL	Rolling on the floor laughing
SYSOP	System Operator
TIA	Thanks in advance

spam—To attempt to overwhelm an individual with a deluge of messages, in response to some transgression, perceived or real.

subdomain—A subdivision of a domain. (If a university's computer network is considered a domain, a computer system in one department of that university would be considered a subdomain. A single computer on the network could also be considered a subdomain, or a sub-subdomain.)

URL—Uniform Resource Locator. The address of a page on the World Wide Web.

Now that you've got the basics down, enjoy the real reason why you picked up this book: the abundance of legal information available on the Internet.

Part Two: The Sites

Have a Problem? Check Here First!

The sites in this first section of Part Two allow you to "help yourself" in a couple of different ways. First, this section presents something of a legal banquet or buffet; there are numerous headings here devoted to particular areas of the law, and you can help yourself to whatever interests you. (Some of the most unique sites are grouped here under the heading "A Miscellany of Interesting Sites.") Second, because the law has many more subject areas than the ones I've arbitrarily listed here, I've also included a special collection of what I call "Smorgasboard Sites"—sites that aim to be *overall* resources for questions about the law. You'll find that collection at the end of this section.

 If you can't find what you need in the sites listed here, be sure to check out my "Best Ways of Finding More and Better Sites" section at the end of Part Two.

YOUR RIGHTS AS AN AMERICAN CITIZEN

Where else to start this section but with help for questions you might have concerning your basic rights.

FUNDAMENTAL DOCUMENTS, AND THE SOURCES OF YOUR RIGHTS

In this first group of sites you will find the fundamental documents of American law—the Constitution and the Declaration of Independence—as well as *The Federalist Papers* and other historical, foundational works.

The Constitution

http://www.law.cornell.edu/constitution/constitution.overview.html

There are many copies of the U.S. Constitution available on the Internet, but most are just text files. None of them is as good as this one, from the Legal Information Institute at the Cornell University School of Law. This hypertext document breaks the Constitution into its component parts so you can jump directly to the text you want without having to scroll around. There are links that take you to the Preamble, to each of the Constitution's seven Articles, to each section of each Article, to the Amendments, and to a list of the signers at the Constitutional Convention. Every link has a label identifying the subject of the linked text, making it possible to find, for example, the "Scope of Legislative Power" (Article I, Section 8), "The Amendment Process" (Article V), and many other interesting topics.

One feature that makes this Constitution particularly useful is that clauses that have been changed or are no longer in effect appear as links that take you to the Amendment(s) that made the changes (Figure 2.1).

Section 3. The Senate of the United States shall be composed of two Senators from each state, chosen by the legislature thereof

, for six years; and each Senator shall have one vote.

Immediately after they shall be assembled in consequence of the first election, they shall be divided as equally as may be into three classes. The seats of the Senators of the first class shall be vacated at the expiration of the second year, of the second class at the expiration of the fourth year, and the third class at the expiration of the sixth year, so that one third may be chosen every second year; and if vacancies happen by resignation, or otherwise, during the recess of the legislature of any state, the executive thereof may make temporary appointments until the next meeting of the legislature, which shall then fill such vacancies.

No person shall be a Senator who shall not have attained to the age of thirty years, and been nine years a citizen of the United States and who shall not, when elected, be an inhabitant of that state for which he shall be chosen.

Amendment XVII

The Senate of the United States shall be composed of two Senators from each state, elected by the people thereof, for six years; and each Senator shall have one vote. The electors in each state shall have the qualifications requisite for electors of the most numerous branch of the state legislatures.

When vacancies happen in the representation of any state in the Senate, the executive authority of such state shall issue writs of election to fill such vacancies: Provided, that the legislature of any state may empower the executive thereof to make temporary appointments until the people fill the vacancies by election as the legislature may direct.

This amendment shall not be so construed as to affect the election or term of any Senator chosen before it becomes valid as part of the Constitution.

Figure 2.1:

Top: Article I Section 3 of the Constitution before it was amended provided that senators be elected by state legislatures. Click on the first underlined link on this page and you are automatically taken to the Seventeenth Amendment, *bottom,* which provides for direct elections of senators.

The Declaration of Independence

ftp.eff.org

The Declaration of Independence is available in many places on the Internet. This particular one is located on the Gopher of the Electronic Frontier Foundation (EFF) in a file called Dec Of Ind, under the menu entries Computers & Academic Freedom archives & info and Civics Archive.

Unlike the outstanding hypertext Constitution in the previous entry, all of the copies of the Declaration I was able to find are straight text files. There isn't, then, much reason for preferring one over another. I selected this site because the EFF has made available a lot of interesting and relevant material along with the Declaration. If you browse a little, you will find a copy of the Constitution, the full text of Thoreau's essay *Civil Disobedience*, and many other, similar documents.

The documents at this site are also available by FTP at the address ftp.eff.org, *in the directory* /pub/CAF/civics.

If you are using a Web browser, you do not have to step through the Gopher menus; you can go directly to the Declaration. Use the URL:

gopher://ftp.eff.org:70/00/CAF/civics/dec_of_ind

It is easier to browse related documents if you go in through the Gopher, however.

The Federalist Papers

http://www.pls.com:8001/d2/kelli/httpd/htdocs/his/8.GBM

The Federalist Papers first appeared in various New York newspapers from the end of 1787 into 1788. Written under the pseudonym Publius and addressed to the People of the State of New York, the papers were an attempt by Alexander Hamilton, James Madison, and John Jay to persuade that state to ratify the new Constitution. Hamilton, Madison, and Jay not only procured ratification, but, to understate the matter somewhat, created documents of lasting importance.

This Web page contains links to sites that arrange *The Federalist Papers* both by number and by name (i.e., subject). Since the papers are often published only by number, the latter arrangement is useful as a guide to content. It would have been better, however, not to alphabetize names that begin with "The" under the letter T.

Finally, if your interest in *The Federalist Papers* is more than casual and you are going to spend any length of time reading them, I would recommend getting your hands on a printed version. There are a total of 85 papers and together they make up a fair size book. Reading that quantity of material for hours and hours on line can be hard on the eyes, and possibly on the pocketbook as well.

More Fundamental Documents

http://www.pls.com:8001/d2/kelli/httpd/htdocs/his/2.GBM

This page is part of the House of Representatives Internet Law Library, a rich resource for legal information on the Internet. As such, it will appear frequently throughout this book as the site for numerous documents of note.

This page collects many links to the Constitution, the Declaration of Independence, and a few of the papers from *The Federalist Papers*, and adds its own links to such materials as the Articles of Confederation, the full text of the most famous works of Thomas Paine, and a few of the works of Thomas Jefferson.

If you follow the links to Constitution and other fundamental documents, and then choose the link Pre-Constitution Documents or Post-Constitution Documents, for example, you will find further links to such items as the Magna Charta, the Mayflower Compact, the Emancipation Proclamation, and the Gettysburg Address. This site is a good source of primary historical documents or just a good place to browse.

Civil Cases v. Criminal Cases

You've probably heard people talk about "criminal law" and "civil law," or "criminal cases" and "civil cases." The difference between civil and criminal often causes a lot of confusion. Here, then, in a nutshell are some important differences.

A civil case is usually initiated and brought directly by a private party. A criminal case can only be brought by the government. If Fred, for example, breaches a contract with Elaine, she could contact an attorney and bring suit herself. If Elaine is the victim of a crime, she must request that the state take action, i.e., by going to the police, and the district attorney has discretion whether or not to prosecute.

In a civil case, one party seeks to compel the other to pay money damages or to compel the other party to take an action or refrain from taking action. In a criminal case, the state seeks fines or a restraint on the defendant's liberty. Elaine could seek money damages from Fred for his breach of their contract, or she might seek "specific performance," an order that Fred perform his contractual obligations. If Fred committed a crime, though, the state would seek to put him in jail or on probation; or it can seek fines, which he pays to the state; or, under limited circumstances, he can be ordered to pay his victim restitution.

Finally, to win a civil case the plaintiff (the party bringing the suit) must prove its case by a "preponderance of the evidence," i.e., it must show that its version of the case is *more-likely-than-not* true. A criminal case requires a much stronger showing than this, because constitutional protection of the defendant's liberty is built in. In order to convict, the prosecution must show that an accused defendant is guilty "beyond a reasonable doubt." Not that he is probably guilty; rather, that the jury is entirely *convinced* of his guilt.

PROTECTING YOUR RIGHTS

The rights of American citizens come not only from the Constitution but from laws like the Civil Rights Act and the Americans with Disabilities Act, among many others. In this section you'll find organizations devoted to helping people protect their legal rights.

American Civil Liberties Union Free Reading Room

aclu.org

From the Gopher menu at this site, choose Society, Law, Politics, and then American Civil Liberties Union to find a mass of information on civil liberties cases from the past and the present, including summaries of Supreme Court briefs, arguments, and decisions. In some cases (noted at the end of the brief) the full text of a brief is available by FTP.

Included is a long list of ACLU position papers on every aspect of Bill of Rights questions, and congressional votes (though not the votes cast by individual members) on civil liberties legislation for the current congress.

If you're using a Web browser you can go directly to the site by using the following URL:

gopher://aclu.org:6601/1

Citizen's Guide to Internet Resources

http://asa.ugl.lib.umich.edu/chdocs/rights/Citizen.html

A bushel of links to Internet resources on the rights of Americans, this site provides connections to information on the rights of women, disabled persons, lesbians, gay men, noncitizen immigrants, the homeless, non-English-speaking persons, and others. There are connections to info on consumer protection, privacy, and other civil rights questions.

BUSINESS AND COMMERCIAL LAW

The Uniform Commerical Code (UCC) site in this section is something I wish I had when I was studying Sales in law school. The UCC governs many different kinds of commercial transactions and has been adopted by every state (and by Washington D.C., The Virgin Islands, and Guam).

The Uniform Commercial Code

http://www.law.cornell.edu/ucc/ucc.table.html

This is a fully searchable, hypertext version of the Uniform Commercial Code (UCC), which regulates many different kinds of commercial transactions. It is another excellent site from the Legal Information Institute at Cornell University. The text of the code is divided into its nine component Articles and these into their component sections, and you can jump directly to any one you need. Every link on the page describes what it links you to, making it easy to find a topic, even if you don't know the structure of the code very well.

Although the Uniform Commercial Code has been adopted in every state, the text of the code in each state is different (if only a little). The UCC as it first appears here is the model drawn up for each state to consider and adapt to suit its own needs and policies. However, the text of the UCC for specific states is also available here. Follow the link For the UCC as enacted by a particular state... *to see these.*

In addition, each Article is WAIS searchable; follow the Article's Full Text Search link to begin the search. You can search for any word or words you like, and the built-in search program will respond with a list of links to the sections that contain what you searched for. For more information on how to compose WAIS searches, see the sidebar *WAIS Searches* in my "Best Ways of Finding More and Better Sites" section at the end of Part Two.

A tip for practitioners: The full text of the Comments to the UCC is available here.

Finally, there are cross-references within the text of most sections. Terms defined in a section other than the one you are reading or references made to other sections appear as links that take you directly to the appropriate definition or section.

A Contract Is Not a Piece of Paper

There is a common misconception people have about contract law—that a contract is a piece of paper. Many assume that if a contract isn't in writing, you can't enforce it or, conversely, that words on a page above a couple of signatures have some magical power to make someone do something. This is not correct.

Rather, a contract, stripped down to its bare bones, is just an agreement or a "meeting of the minds," where each party gives and receives something of value (so-called "consideration"). So, if Fred says to Elaine, I'll give you $1000 if you paint my garage this Saturday, and Elaine says okay, they've made a contract. Fred and Elaine agree on what they both will do, and each gives and receives something of value: Fred promises to give $1000 and gets a promise to have his garage painted; Elaine promises her painting services and gets a promise of $1000. This is an enforceable contract whether or not Elaine and Fred write their agreement down.

Why, then, do people insist upon writing contracts down (and rightly so)? Because the written agreement is *evidence* of the existence and the terms of the contract, if you have to sue to enforce it. If Fred refuses to pay Elaine after she paints his garage and she sues him for her money, it's simply easier for Elaine to prove her case if she can show the court a signed written agreement.

All of this said, however, some contracts must be in writing to be enforceable (contracts made in contemplation of marriage, real estate contracts, contracts for the sale of goods more than $500, and a few others), and some contracts can't be enforced even if they are written down (contracts to do something illegal or against public policy, such a a contract for sex).

CONSUMER PROTECTION

The sites in this section provide a wealth of useful consumer information. If you have a credit card, are thinking about buying or leasing a car, are concerned about the safety of products made for young children, or have any other consumer concern, you'll be interested in what you can find here.

The Better Business Bureau

http://www.igc.apc.org:80/cbbb/

This site is a great consumer reference. The Better Business Bureau provides information here on the services that it offers through its local branches nationwide. For example, it tells you how to make an inquiry or file a complaint about misleading advertising, how to find alternative ways to resolve disputes between businesses and consumers (e.g., arbitration), how to find out about charities, where to find reports on a business's reliability, and more (Figure 2.2).

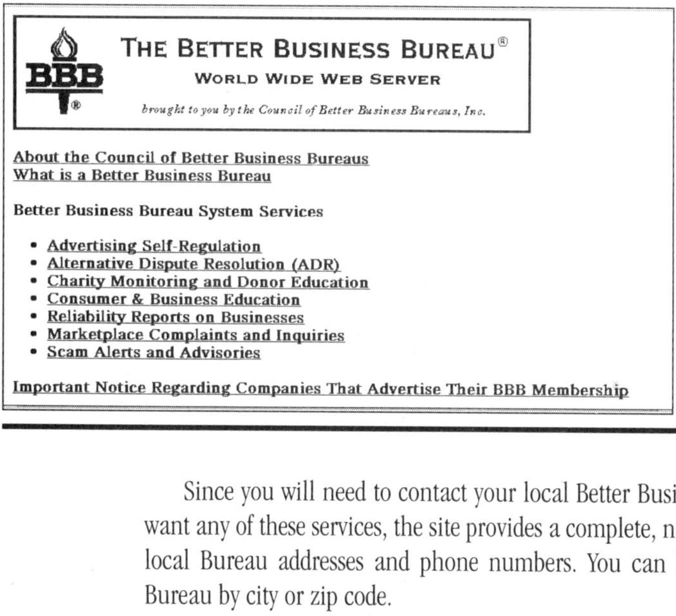

THE BETTER BUSINESS BUREAU®
WORLD WIDE WEB SERVER
brought to you by the Council of Better Business Bureaus, Inc.

About the Council of Better Business Bureaus
What is a Better Business Bureau

Better Business Bureau System Services

- Advertising Self-Regulation
- Alternative Dispute Resolution (ADR)
- Charity Monitoring and Donor Education
- Consumer & Business Education
- Reliability Reports on Businesses
- Marketplace Complaints and Inquiries
- Scam Alerts and Advisories

Important Notice Regarding Companies That Advertise Their BBB Membership

Figure 2.2:
The Better Business Bureau WWW Page. Underlined links at the top of the page describe the services the BBB offers.

Since you will need to contact your local Better Business Bureau if you want any of these services, the site provides a complete, national directory of local Bureau addresses and phone numbers. You can look up your own Bureau by city or zip code.

You can also find here a number of consumer information publications (full-text) available on a variety of subjects.

The Massachusetts Executive Office of Consumer Affairs and Business Regulation

http://www.tiac.net:80/consumer/

Below this mouthful of a title is a genuinely useful Web page, which allows the user to file a consumer complaint, submit a question about consumer rights, and read or order consumer information booklets, all on line.

Complaints can be filed only by Massachusetts residents or against Massachusetts businesses, and the Office will only answer questions about Massachusetts consumer law.

Many of the booklets provide information useful to everyone and they cover topics such as how to get a copy of your credit report and how to prevent your credit card issuer from taking advantage of you (Figure 2.3).

Read Booklets Online

Click on the title of the booklet below that you wish to read.
- ☐ New Car Lemon Law
- ☐ Used Car Lemon Law
- ☐ Lemon Aid Law
- ☐ Landlord/Tenant Rights
- ☐ How to Get a Copy of Your Credit Report
- ☐ How to Write a 30 Day Demand Letter
- ☐ A Consumer Guide to the Home Improvement Contractor Law
- ☐ 12 Credit Card Secrets Banks Don't Want You to Know
- ☐ Description of the Executive Office of Consumer Affairs
- ☐ Questions and Answers about Life Insurance (e-text only)
- ☐ Questions and Answers about Health Insurance (e-text only)
- ☐ Questions and Answers about Homeowners Insurance (e-text)
- ☐ Questions and Answers about Long Term Care Insurance (e-text)
- ☐ Questions & Answers about Workers' Compensation (e-text only)
- ☐ Q&A about Workers' Compensation (Employer's Guide) (e-text)
- ☐ Questions & Answers about Auto Insurance (e-text only)

If you have any questions, please send mail to *ask@consumer.com* or use the provided comment form. We hope you've found this service valuable.

Figure 2.3:
The Massachusetts Executive Office of Consumer Affairs and Business Regulation provides consumer information booklets on line.

In order to file a complaint, ask a question, or order a booklet on line, you must have a Web browser (such as Netscape or Mosaic) that supports online forms. If your browser does not support online forms, the page provides forms that you can print out and send in by postal mail.

The Consumer Law Page™

http://tsw.ingress.com/tsw/talf/txt/intro.html

This page, produced by the Alexander Law Firm of San Jose, California, is quite a valuable source of consumer information. In addition to links to other consumer information on the Internet, you will also find more than 100 consumer information brochures that you can read.

The brochures cover a wide variety of subjects of interest to the consumer, such as (to name only a very few) truth in automobile leasing, your rights when an error appears on your credit card bill, how to spot telemarketing fraud, and even what to ask when selecting a plastic surgeon. If you have a question about your consumer rights, take a look here.

The Consumer Product Safety Commission

cpsc.gov

The Consumer Product Safety Commission (CPSC) is the federal agency assigned to "protect the public against unreasonable risks of injuries and deaths associated with consumer products." The CPCS Gopher is a clearinghouse for useful information about the Commission and its activities.

You will find at this site information about the CPSC, how it works and how to contact it to report an unsafe product. You will also find an archive of news releases and announcements about product recalls and safety information.

Anyone who wishes to receive current Consumer Product Safety Commission information can subscribe to the CPSC list mailing. Just send an e-mail message (with no subject line) saying

sub CPSCINFO-L Yourfirstname Yourlastname

to listproc@cpsc.gov. You will then receive CPSC news releases and announcements by electronic mail until you unsubscribe from the list.

COPYRIGHT, PATENTS, AND TRADEMARKS

As a medium rich with the possibility of copying original material over and over again, the Internet itself gives rise to questions about copyright and intellectual property. In this section you'll find sites with information concerning copyright, patents, and trademarks, and intellectual property law in general.

COPYRIGHT LAW

Basic Copyright Information

marvel.loc.gov

If you have a basic copyright question, why not get your answers right from the source? At this site, under the menu entry Copyright you will find a file called Copyright Basics (Circular 1). This file, which contains the full text (about 40,000 bytes) of a United States Copyright Office circular, provides an excellent overview of copyrights. The circular explains in fairly general terms and without too much legalese what a copyright is, who can claim one, what kinds of things you can and cannot copyright, how long copyright protection lasts, and how to copyright ("register") a work, and so forth.

If you are using a Web browser you do not have to step through the Gopher menus to get to the circular. You can go directly there by using the URL:

gopher://marvel.loc.gov:70/00/copyright/circs/circ01

If you want to know how to register a copyright, this is the place to look for instruction.

The U.S. Copyright Office Gopher

marvel.loc.gov

You'll find the United States Copyright Office gopher (actually a part of the Library of Congress gopher, hence the address), under the menu entry Copyright.

If you are using a Web browser, you can go directly to the Copyright Office gopher. Use the URL:

gopher://marvel.loc.gov:70/11/copyright

The Copyright Office makes available here a lot of general information about copyrights (See the previous entry for basic copyright information). The heading In Answer to Your Query (Form Letters) contains what are essentially Copyright Office FAQ's, such as "What is fair use?" and "Can you copyright a photograph?" Under the menu entry Copyright Information Circulars, you'll find still more information, some of it fairly detailed (see Figure 2.4).

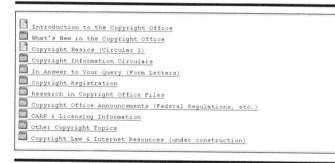

Figure 2.4:
The Copyright Office Gopher offers a lot of information about copyrights.

Unfortunately, to get copyright registration forms, you must call or write the offices you'll find listed through this site; it does not make the forms available for download.

A Copyright List Mailer

This list mailing is a product of the Coalition for Networked Information. It is intended as a forum where subscribers may "ask, answer, and discuss copyright questions of any type." In the short time I subscribed to this mailing, I found the level of discussion quite high. The questions posed were interesting, thoughtful, and well considered, as were the answers, and the discussion never drifted off into irrelevant tangents as so often happens in list mailings and newsgroups. The discussions were, moreover, polite—there were no flames or name calling.

To subscribe, send the message:

subscribe cni-copyright yourfirstname yourlastname

to listproc@cni.org. Send messages you want to post to cni-copyright@cni.org.

Title 17 of the U.S. Code: The Copyright Law

http://www.law.cornell.edu/usc/17/overview.html

This is the Cornell Legal Information Institute's fully searchable, hypertext version of Title 17 of the United States Code, the copyright law. It is excellent. The text of the law is broken into its component sections, and you can jump directly to any one you need. Every link on the page describes what it links you to, making it possible to find a topic, even if you don't at first know where it's located.

Practitioners should note that there are no annotations or comments, only descriptions of what is linked to what. Therefore, this site is most useful as a reference and not so much as a research tool.

Title 17 as presented here is also WAIS searchable; follow the Full Text Search link to search (you can search for any word or words you like, and the built-in search program will respond with a list of links to the sections that contain what you searched for).

Finally, there are cross-references within the text of each section. Terms defined in a section other than the one you are reading or references made to other sections appear as links that take you directly to the appropriate definition or section (Figure 2.5).

U.S. COPYRIGHT ACT, AS AMENDED
..CHAPTER 3. DURATION OF COPYRIGHT

---

§ 302. Duration of copyright: Works created on or after January 1, 1978

- **(a) In general**
- Copyright in a work created on or after January 1, 1978, subsists from its creation and, except as provided by the following subsections, endures for a term consisting of the life of the author and fifty years after the author's death.
- **(b) Joint works**
- In the case of a joint work prepared by two or more authors who did not work for hire, the copyright endures for a term consisting of the life of the last surviving author and fifty years after such last surviving author's death.
- **(c) Anonymous works, pseudonymous works, and works made for hire**
- In the case of an anonymous work, a pseudonymous work, or a work made for hire, the copyright endures for a term of seventy-five years from the year of its first publication, or a term of one hundred years from the year of its creation, whichever expires first. If, before the end of such term, the identity of one or more of the authors of an anonymous or pseudonymous work is revealed in the records of a registration made for that work under subsections (a) or (d) of section 408 [17 USCS § 408], or in the records provided by this subsection, the copyright in the work endures for the term specified by subsection (a) or (b), based on the life of the author or authors whose identity has been revealed. Any person having an interest in the copyright in an anonymous or pseudonymous work may at any time record, in records to be maintained by the Copyright Office for that purpose, a

A "joint work" is a work prepared by two or more authors with the intention that their contributions be merged into inseparable or interdependent parts of a unitary whole.

"Literary works" are works, other than audiovisual works, expressed in words, numbers, or other verbal or numerical symbols or indicia, regardless of the nature of the material objects, such as books, periodicals, manuscripts, phonorecords, film, tapes, disks, or cards, in which they are embodied.

"Motion pictures" are audiovisual works consisting of a series of related images which, when shown in succession, impart an impression of motion, together with accompanying sounds, if any.

To "perform" a work means to recite, render, play, dance, or act it, either directly or by means of any device or process or, in the case of a motion picture or other audiovisual work, to show its images in any sequence or to make the sounds accompanying it audible.

"Phonorecords" are material objects in which sounds, other than those accompanying a motion picture or other audiovisual work, are fixed by any method now known or later developed, and from which the sounds can be perceived, reproduced, or otherwise communicated, either directly or with the aid of a machine or device. The term "phonorecords" includes the material object in which the sounds are first fixed.

"Pictorial, graphic, and sculptural works" include two-dimensional and three-dimensional works of fine, graphic, and applied art, photographs, prints and art reproductions, maps, globes, charts, diagrams, models, and technical drawings, including architectural plans. Such works shall include works of artistic craftsmanship insofar as their form but not their mechanical or utilitarian aspects are concerned; the design of a useful article, as defined in this section, shall be considered a pictorial, graphic, or sculptural

Figure 2.5:
Top: Part of Section 302 of the U.S. Copyright Act. Notice that some terms and cross-references are links. Click on *joint work* and you arrive at the part of Section 101 of the Copyright Act that defines "joint work" (*bottom*).

PATENT LAW

The U.S. Patent and Trademark Office

http://www.uspto.gov/

The U.S. Patent and Trademark Office's Web page contains links to information about the Office, links to collaborative online projects, and information about recent changes in patent law, among other things. There are also links to basic patent and trademark information.

The patent information tells you, among other things, what a patent is, what kinds of things you can patent, what the elements of a patent application are, and so forth. Similarly, the trademark information tells you about the requirements for filing a trademark application and provides a list of phone numbers for further information.

If you have some basic patent and trademark questions, this is a good place to start looking for answers.

Full-Text Patent Searches

http://town.hall.org/patent/patent.html

The full text of patents issued from January 1, 1994 is available at this site from the Internet Multicasting Service. The patents are searchable; in fact, you must run a search to see any of them. Just enter key words and the built-in search program returns a list of links to the patents that contain the terms you searched for.

This site is of some use to anyone who wants to do a search for recent patents. If I could make a wish, I would ask for images (currently they aren't included with the patent text). I'd also like to see patents from earlier than 1994.

Full-Text Patent Searches II

http://sunsite.unc.edu/patents/intropat.html

This site makes available abstracts for patents issued from 1984 through 1989, and the titles of patents issued from 1970 to the present. This site does not provide the full text of any of the patents, however; so this site is of limited use.

To search for a particular patent abstract, you have to find the patent number, which you can retrieve from a title search. To search for a patent title, you must first determine the class and subclass numbers the Patent and Trademark Office assigns to inventions. Fortunately, the site provides an index and master list of those classes.

This site would be more useful if more abstracts were available and if searching could be done by keywords as well as by patent number and class.

The Patent Act: Title 35 of the U.S. Code

http://www.law.cornell.edu/usc/35/i_iv/overview.html

This is a fully searchable, hypertext version of Title 35 of the United States Code, better known as the Patent Act, from the Legal Information Institute at Cornell University. It is an excellent site. The text of the act is broken down into its component sections and you can jump directly to any section you need. Every link on the page describes what it links you to, making it possible to find a topic even if you don't at first know where it's located.

Practitioners should note that there are no annotations or comments available, only descriptions of what is linked to what. Therefore, this site is most useful as a reference and not so much as a research tool.

Alternatively, you can find what you want by searching, since the act as presented here is WAIS searchable. Just follow the Full Text Search link. (You can search for any word or words you like, and the built-in search program will respond with a list of links to the sections that contain what you searched for.)

Finally, there are cross-references within the text of most sections. Terms defined in a section other than the one you are reading or references made to other sections appear as links that take you directly to the appropriate definition or section (Figure 2.6).

U.S. PATENT ACT, AS AMENDED
..PART II. PATENTABILITY OF INVENTIONS AND GRANT OF PATENTS
....CHAPTER 11. APPLICATION FOR PATENT

§ 114. Models, specimens

The Commissioner may require the applicant to furnish a model of convenient size to exhibit advantageously the several parts of his invention.

When the invention relates to a composition of matter, the Commissioner may require the applicant to furnish specimens or ingredients for the purpose of inspection or experiment.

U.S. PATENT ACT, AS AMENDED
..PART II. PATENTABILITY OF INVENTIONS AND GRANT OF PATENTS
....CHAPTER 10. PATENTABILITY OF INVENTIONS

§ 100. Definitions

When used in this title [35 USCS §§ 1 et seq.] unless the context otherwise indicates-

- (a) The term "**invention**" means invention or discovery.
- (b) The term "**process**" means process, art or method, and includes a new use of a known process, machine, manufacture, composition of matter, or material.
- (c) The terms "**United States**" and "**this country**" mean the United States of America, its territories and possessions.
- (d) The word "**patentee**" includes not only the patentee to whom the patent was issued but also the successors in title to the patentee.

Figure 2.6:
Top: Section 114 of the U.S. Patent Act uses the word "invention," which appears as a link. Click on it and you jump to Section 100, *bottom*, which defines the term as it is used in the act.

TRADEMARK LAW

A Summary of U.S. Trademark Law

http://www.law.cornell.edu:80/topics/trademark.html

This page contains a good short summary of U.S. trademark law. It defines trademarks, the kind of protection available under the law, and so forth. What makes the page noteworthy, though, are the links within the summary text. When the summary discusses a section of the Lanham Act (i.e., the Trademark Law) or the Constitution, there is a link in the text that takes you directly to the the law discussed (Figure 2.7).

Trademark Law Materials

Trademarks are generally distinctive symbols, pictures, or words that sellers affix to distinguish and identify the origin of their products. Trademark status may also be granted to distinctive and unique packaging, color combinations, building designs, product styles, and overall presentations. It is also possible to receive trademark status for identification that is not on its face distinct or unique but which has developed a secondary meaning over time that identifies it with the product or seller. The owner of a trademark has exclusive right to use it on the product it was intended to identify and often on related products. Service-marks receive the same legal protection as trademarks but are meant to distinguish services rather than products.

In the United States trademarks may be protected by both Federal statute under the Lanham Act, 15 U.S.C. § § 1051 - 1127, and a state's statutory and/or common law. Congress enacted the Lanham Act under its Constitutional grant of authority to regulate interstate and foreign commerce. *See* U.S. Constitution, Article 1, Section 8, Clause 3. A trademark registered under the Lanham Act has nationwide protection. *See* § 1115 of the Act.

Under the Lanham Act, a seller applies to the Patent and Trademark Office to register a trademark. The mark can already be in use or be one that will be used in the future. *See* § 1051 of the act. The Office's regulations pertaining to trademarks are found in Parts 1 - 7 of Title 37 of the Code of Federal Regulations. If the trademark is initially, approved by an examiner, it is published in the Official Gazette of the Trademark Office to notify other parties of the pending approval so that it may be opposed. *See* § § 1062 - 1063 of the Act. An appeals process is available for rejected applications. *See* § § 1070 - 1071 of the Act.

Figure 2.7:
Part of the discussion of trademark law. Notice the links which will take you to the Lanham Act and the Constitution.

The discussion of trademark law here is one of a number of such discussions prepared by the Cornell Legal Information Institute. See the Law Summaries entry under the heading "Best 'Smorgasboard Sites': Sites with Everything!" later in this section.

As an added bonus, the page contains links to trademark information at other Internet sites.

If you want to reach the text of the U.S. trademark law directly, see its entry below, The Lanham Act: U.S. Trademark Law.

Trademark Application Forms

http://www.naming.com/naming/tmforms.html

This page is part of a site maintained by Master-McNeil, a Berkeley, California provider of "product and corporate naming services." They have made available the main trademark application form, as well as supplementary forms that you might need, in .TIF and .GIF formats. You can download the .TIF files if you have a program that can display and print them. If you don't, use your Web browser to display and print the forms.

The Lanham Act: U.S. Trademark Law

http://www.law.cornell.edu:80/usc/15/22/overview.html

This is a fully searchable, hypertext version of the Lanham Act, the U.S. trademark law, from the Legal Information Institute at Cornell University. It is an excellent site. The text of the act is broken down into its component sections and you can jump directly to any section you need (Figure 2.8). Every link on the page describes what it links you to, making it possible to find major topics quickly without having to carry out a search.

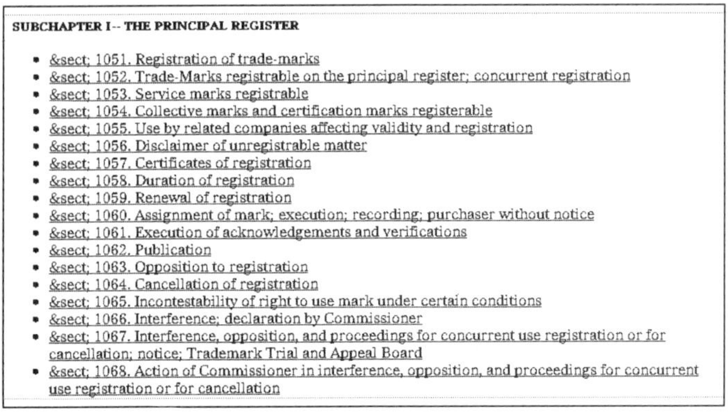

SUBCHAPTER I-- THE PRINCIPAL REGISTER

- § 1051. Registration of trade-marks
- § 1052. Trade-Marks registrable on the principal register; concurrent registration
- § 1053. Service marks registrable
- § 1054. Collective marks and certification marks registerable
- § 1055. Use by related companies affecting validity and registration
- § 1056. Disclaimer of unregistrable matter
- § 1057. Certificates of registration
- § 1058. Duration of registration
- § 1059. Renewal of registration
- § 1060. Assignment of mark; execution; recording; purchaser without notice
- § 1061. Execution of acknowledgements and verifications
- § 1062. Publication
- § 1063. Opposition to registration
- § 1064. Cancellation of registration
- § 1065. Incontestability of right to use mark under certain conditions
- § 1066. Interference; declaration by Commissioner
- § 1067. Interference, opposition, and proceedings for concurrent use registration or for cancellation; notice; Trademark Trial and Appeal Board
- § 1068. Action of Commissioner in interference, opposition, and proceedings for concurrent use registration or for cancellation

Figure 2.8:
Some links to sections
of the Lanham Act

Alternatively, you can find what you want by searching, since the act as presented here is WAIS searchable. Just follow the Full Text Search link. (You can search for any word or words you like, and the built-in search program will respond with a list of links to the sections that contain what you searched for.)

Finally, there are cross-references within the text of most sections. Terms defined in a section other than the one you are reading or references made to other sections appear as links that take you directly to the appropriate definition or section.

Practitioners should note that there are no annotations or comments available, so this site is most useful as a reference and not so much as a research tool.

INTELLECTUAL PROPERTY LAW

Legal Care For Your Software

http://www.island.com/LegalCare/welcome.html

This site contains the full text of the Fifth Edition of *Legal Care for Your Software*, "a step-by-step legal guide for computer software writers, programmers, and publishers."

If you're any one of the above, you'll find a good deal of useful and practical information here. The book tells you in clear language what kinds of legal protection are available to you—copyright and trade secrets, for example—and how you go about obtaining them. It is also instructive about contracts and contract law, devoting a number of chapters to the kinds of contracts you might need, such as work-for-hire agreements, licensing agreements, and beta test agreements.

If you're more comfortable with a book in your hand than on your screen, you'll find instructions for ordering a copy.

IP Magazine

http://www.portal.com/~recorder/intro.html

IP Magazine is a quarterly publication of *The Recorder*, a San Francisco legal newspaper. The magazine says it covers the latest "developments in the laws governing technology and information, from federal copyright law to the protection of trade secrets to antitrust enforcement," and it does so with an eye always on business.

I found the magazine's coverage to be even broader than this description might lead you to believe. In one recent issue alone, articles were about such diverse topics as ways for in-house lawyers and outside counsel to communicate effectively, stock offerings in technology companies, and the consequences of universities seeking to make money from the fruits of their research.

IP Magazine *is available in printed as well as electronic form.*

A Law and Computing Newsgroup

misc.legal.computing

This is a general-purpose newsgroup that deals with the things that go on at the intersection of law and computers. There are, for example, frequent discussions of software patents and of copyright issues raised by the World Wide Web. These are merely representative examples, though, for the subjects discussed are quite broad, as is the range of interested participants, who include in their numbers attorneys and computer industry professionals.

ENTERTAINMENT LAW

The U.S. is peppered with aspiring filmmakers and screenwriters. If you've always wanted to go into show business, you'll need to brush up on entertainment legalities. Here's an interesting site to help you do that.

Entertainment Law CyberCenter

http://www.hollywoodnetwork.com/Law/

On this home page for Hollywood dealmaker Mark Litwin, you'll find excerpts from his books covering film and television agreements. Self-defense tips for filmmakers, screenwriters, and producers give you an insight into "the art of the deal" as it applies in tinseltown. Worth a visit, if only to learn how a hit movie can fail to turn a profit.

Lawyer Jokes

Q: Why are lawyers like nuclear weapons?

A: If one side has one, the other side has to get one. Once launched during a campaign, they can rarely be recalled. And when they land, they screw up everything forever.

If you like lawyer jokes as I do, though I'm not certain that all lawyers do, then you'll want to take a look at Nolo Press's lawyer joke page, where I got this joke. Some of the jokes are really very funny and the list is constantly growing. Nolo is always on the lookout for more lawyer jokes and you are invited to contribute.

Nolo is not the only Internet collector of lawyer jokes. You should also try the University of Texas Law School collection at
http://deputy.law.utexas.edu/jokes1.htm
and also at
http://deputy.law.utexas.edu/jokes2.htm

ENVIRONMENTAL LAW

Currently a growing field of practice, environmental law is also growing on the Internet. The two sites in this section will take you to much of what is environmental on the Internet.

The WWW Virtual Law Library: Environmental Law

http://www.law.indiana.edu/law/intenvlaw.html

This page is a part of the Virtual Law Library from the Indiana University School of Law (see The WWW Virtual Law Library: Law entry under the heading "Best 'Smorgasboard Sites': Sites with Everything!"). It contains a long alphabetical list of links to a wide variety of sites related to environmental law.

You will find links to U.S. environmental laws such as the Clean Air Act, to international environmental treaties such as the Convention on International Trade in Endangered Species, and to environmental and scientific organizations around the world, both in government and in the private sector.

The Green Page

http://www.echonyc.com/~kamml/enviro.html

This page, like the entry for The WWW Virtual Law Library: Environmental Law above, casts a very wide net. I include it here because it complements the Virtual Law Library environmental page very well.

This page has links to sites with scientific information on the environment and to sites with information about environmentally friendly products. In addition, of course, there are links to sites about environmental law. If you began looking for environmental law information at the WWW Virtual Law Library (above), consider continuing your search here.

FAMILY LAW

The sites in this section provide useful family law information, from how a divorce proceeding works to how to seek federal help in enforcing child support.

LEGAL.NET™

http://www.legal.net/

Pronounced "legal dot net," this site has a number of nice features—about family law and otherwise—that make it worth a visit. There are, for example, articles on various topics written by attorneys who practice in the area they're writing about, self-help software you can order, and a directory of attorneys.

If you're interested in family law, you'll find an article that spells out, step-by-step, how a divorce proceeding works. You can also order software to calculate the amount of child or spousal support you owe or that is owed to you. (Note, however, that the child/spousal support calculation software is for use in California only.)

One of the best features of LEGAL.NET is "Dear Esquire," where anyone who wishes may post legal questions for attorneys to answer. If you have a question about family law, or about anything for that matter, consider posting it here.

The Administration for Children and Families

http://www.acf.dhhs.gov/

The Administration for Children and Families (ACF) is part of the Department of Health and Human Services. Its purpose is to "promote the economic and social well-being of families, children, individuals, and communities." This is quite a broad mandate, and as such, ACF administers a number of different programs, including Head Start and At-Risk Child Care. Although general information about all ACF programs is available here, at the time of this writing additional specific and practical information was available for only one of the Administration's programs. All of which goes to say that this site is still under construction.

The one ACF program for which additional information was available is The Office of Child Support Enforcement, and what is given is quite important. You will find information about how to apply for enforcement services, the procedures involved in collecting support, and a national directory of CSE offices. Information about state child-support programs is also available.

IMMIGRATION LAW

Most of the sites addressing immigration law as it applies in relation to the United States are run by individual law firms. Even so, there's lots of good basic information in these sites. Be aware that anything you read on this topic must be confirmed before you make any plans, because of the rapidly changing nature of immigration rules.

Canadian to U.S. Immigration FAQ

http://www.grasmick.com/canimfaq.htm

If you're a Canadian considering immigration to the United States either temporarily or permanently, check out this site, which provides information in the form of questions and answers. Turn here to learn about the kinds of visas and work permits used by Canadians in the U.S., and about their availability and limitations. You'll also find tips on how to find a Canadian immigration lawyer, and the pros and cons of dual citizenship.

Citizenship and Immigration Canada

http://www.ingenia.com/cicnet/english/index.html

This is the English-language home page of the Canadian Department of Citizenship and Immigration. It includes links to information on citizenship and how to get it. Also available are documents on immigration policy and procedures, downloadable in WordPerfect 5.1 format.

Questions and Answers on Dual US/Other Citizenship

http://www.mks.com/~richw/dualcit.html#QandA

A page with lots of answers to questions concerning dual citizenship, including specific references to issues of living abroad, foreign military service, and maintaining two passports at the same time. The entries are succinct but complete.

Siskind's Immigration Bulletin

http://www.telalink.net/~gsiskind/bulletin.html

In this monthly newsletter written by immigration lawyers addressing nuts-and-bolts immigration issues, you'll find things like the exact amount of time it takes for a given INS office to process applications (each issue has information on several offices), visa availability by country, and updates on current and pending legislation. All the information is specific and quite timely.

Immigration Newsgroups on Usenet

The most timely information on immigration issues can often be gleaned from immigration newsgroups. Here's a list of active ones:

alt.visa.us

misc.immigration.usa

can.legal

misc.immigration.canada

misc.immigration.misc

clari.news.immigration

SELF HELP

The sites in this section provide you with a number of different ways to help yourself, from making a Freedom of Information Act request to finding a lawyer.

Legal Latin for the Layperson

ad hoc "for this." An ad hoc committee is named, or an ad hoc appointment is made, for a single, specific purpose.

ad hominem "to the person." An ad hominem argument attacks an opponent personally and not the merits of his position or argument.

arguendo "for the sake of argument." Judges and attorneys will write: "Assuming, arguendo, that...."

certiorari, (writ of) "to be informed of." The writ of certiorari is the means by which the Supreme Court of the United States chooses the cases it wishes to hear. See the sidebar *Getting A Case Before the U.S. Supreme Court* on pg. 126.

de facto "from the fact," and meaning "actual, but not in accordance with the law." Thus a de facto government actually exercises power but was not legally established. In school desegregation cases, de facto segregation is that which comes about unintentionally, not by the actions of the state or school board. Used in contrast to *de jure.*

de jure "by right" or "of right." A de jure government is one that was established in accordance with the law. In school desegregation cases, de jure segregation is that which is intentionally brought about by the state or school board. Used in contrast to *de facto.*

ex benedict Poached eggs with ham and hollandaise sauce on an English muffin.

ex parte "on the part of one party (and not the other)." Usually used to refer to a motion or hearing that is made by or involving only one party in a case.

ex post facto "after the fact." The Constitution, Article I, Section 9 prohibits ex post facto laws: "No bill of attainder or ex post facto Law shall be passed." In its most basic form, this means that Congress cannot pass laws that criminalize actions that, when done, were legal; Congress cannot criminalize actions retroactively

guardian ad litem An attorney appointed by the court to represent the interests of a minor, infant, or unborn child during a case.

habeas corpus (writ of) "You have the body." The writ of habeas corpus is used to attack the legality or constitutionality of a person's imprisonment.

in camera "in chambers." An in camera hearing takes place not in open court but privately in the judge's chambers.

inter alia   "among other things."

ipso facto   "by the fact itself." As in "That, ipso facto, is insufficient; more is required."

j.n.o.v.   *judgement non obstante veredicto* ("judgment notwithstanding the verdict"). A j.n.o.v. motion is one made to the court asking the judge to rule in the favor of the moving party, even though the jury ruled against it.

nolo contendere   "I do not wish to contest." A plea similar to a plea of guilty where you do not admit or deny the crimes you are charged with, but you are still subject to penalty.

non sequitur   "It does not follow." An assertion that doesn't follow logically from anything that came before it.

obiter dicta   "said in passing." Any part of judicial opinion not necessary for the resolution of the case before the court.

prima facie   "on first appearance."

pro bono   Short for *pro bono publico*: "for the public good." If an attorney takes a case pro bono, it means they are taking it without pay.

res ipsa loquitur   "The thing speaks for itself." A doctrine that allows a party to establish a defendant's negligence from the fact of the plaintiff's injury alone (the thing that speaks for itself) when a particular set of circumstances applies.

res judicata   "a judged matter." A rule that prohibits parties from re-litigating a claim or cause of action once it has been finally adjudicated.

sine qua non   "without which not." Something essential or necessary.

subpoena ad testificandum   An order to appear and testify. Usually just called a subpoena.

subpoena colada   An order for a drink with pineapple juice, coconut juice, and rum. Sometimes served with a small, paper umbrella.

subpoena duces tecum   An order to appear and produce documents.

A Citizen's Guide to the Freedom of Information Act

gopher.eff.org

A Citizen's Guide to the Freedom of Information Act (FOIA) is a 1993 report of the House Committee on Government Operations; Subcommittee on Information, Justice, Transportation, and Agriculture. It is available on this Gopher server from the Electronic Frontier Foundation under the entries Electronic Frontier Foundation files & information, then Legislation and regulation relevant to the Electronic Frontier, then Legal, FOIA, and finally foia.guide.

If you're using a Web browser, you can go directly to the *Citizen's Guide* and avoid stepping through the menu entries entirely. Use the URL:

gopher://gopher.eff.org:70/11/EFF/Legislation/Legal/FOIA/foia.guide

FOIA gives individuals the right to obtain documents held by federal agencies and by departments of the executive branch. The range of information that you can request is really quite broad (think about how many agencies and departments there are). Newspapers and researchers make requests frequently, and there is nothing to stop an interested private individual from doing so as well.

The *Citizen's Guide* tells you everything you need to know about how to use FOIA and the related Privacy Act of 1974, which government entities you can make requests of and which ones you can't, what you can request, how you go about requesting it, and why a request may be denied. Making an FOIA request is as simple as writing a letter, and the *Citizen's Guide* provides you with a number of sample letters that you can use as models for your own.

The EFF also makes available an FOIA kit of their own (under the entry foia.kit) which is a guide to the Freedom of Information Act that is similar to the Citizen's Guide but which has additional explanations and many more sample letters you can use as models.

The Social Security Administration

http://www.ssa.gov/SSA_Home.html

The Social Security Administration (SSA) has made available a lot of useful, if not absolutely crucial, information at this site. You'll find, among other things, answers to frequently asked questions such as How do I get a social security number?, How do I replace a lost or stolen social security card?, and How do I notify the SSA of a change of address? There is information for employers about wage reporting and even a copy of the *SSA Handbook*, which is a summary of SSA benefits and policies.

There are a few SSA forms available for download; hopefully there will be more soon. On the Forms Page, you can download the application for a social security card (Figure 2.9) and the form you need to check your earnings record (the Request for Earnings and Benefits Estimate Statement). Under Employer Information, you'll find the form to request an Employer Information Number, which you'll need if you are starting a business.

SOCIAL SECURITY ADMINISTRATION
Application for a Social Security Card

Inside is the form you need to apply for a Social Security card. You can also use this form to replace a lost card or to change your name on your card. This service is free. But before you go on to the form, please read through the rest of this page. We want to cover some facts you should know before you apply.

IF YOU HAVE NEVER HAD A SOCIAL SECURITY NUMBER	If you were born in the U.S. and have never had a Social Security number, you must complete this form and show us documents that show your age, citizenship, and who you are. Usually, all we need from you are: • Your birth certificate; AND • Some form of identity, such as a driver's license, school record, or medical record. See page 2 for more examples. We prefer to see your birth certificate. However, we will accept a hospital record of your birth made before you were 5 years old, or a religious record of your age or birth made before you were 3 months old. We must see original documents or certified copies. Uncertified photocopies are not acceptable. You may apply at any age, but if you are 18 or older when you apply for your first Social Security card, you must apply in person. Please see the special requirements on page 4 if you were born outside the U.S., if you are not a U.S. citizen or if you need a card for a child.
IF YOU NEED TO REPLACE YOUR CARD	To replace your card, all we usually need is one type of identification and this completed form. See page 2 for examples of documents we will accept. If you were born outside the U.S., you must also submit proof of U.S. citizenship or lawful alien status. Examples of the documents we will accept are on page 4. Remember, we must see original documents or certified copies.

Figure 2.9:
Part of the instruction page of the Social Security Administration Application for a social security card

The forms are in .PDF format, which means you will need the Adobe Acrobat reader to print them. See the sidebar *You Can Read Real Forms with the Adobe Acrobat Reader*, nearby.

You Can Read Real Forms with the Adobe Acrobat Reader

The Social Security Administration and the IRS make their forms available to the public over the Internet. The forms come in a number of formats, among them Adobe Acrobat format, which uses the file extension .PDF. One striking feature of files in this format is that you can read them on any system—Windows, DOS, Macintosh, or UNIX—and print them on any printer (except daisy wheels) regardless of what kind of system they were created on. All you need is the Adobe Acrobat Reader, which will allow you to read and print, though not create, files in .PDF format.

The reader is available for download at no cost from its creator, Adobe Systems. You can find it at the Adobe FTP site at:

ftp.adobe.com

in the /pub/adobe/Acrobat directory, or at the Adobe Web page at:

http://www.adobe.com/Software.html

The reader is available in Windows (1.4Mb), DOS (2.5Mb), Macintosh (2Mb), and UNIX (6Mb) formats. The file sizes are large, so it may take you some time to download what you need.

More and more government forms are becoming available on the Internet, and .PDF format is fast becoming a de facto standard.

Nolo Press

http://nearnet.gnn.com/gnn/bus/nolo/

Nolo Press is a Berkeley, California publisher of self-help legal information, books, and software on solving for yourself many common legal problems in such areas as wills, divorce, and landlord/tenant disputes. A complete title and price list is available and you can order on line if you wish.

There are also more than thirty articles that you can read on line about common legal needs, such as answers to frequently asked questions about incorporating, what a living trust is and why you would or wouldn't want one, and how to deal with noisy neighbors. If you're a do-it-yourselfer, check out Nolo Press.

West's Legal Directory of Lawyers and Law Firms

http://www.westpub.com/WLDInfo/WLD.htm

This is a directory of lawyers and law firms from one of the largest (if not *the* largest) legal publisher in the U.S. The directory lists attorneys and firms in all fifty states, plus Washington D.C., Puerto Rico, the U.S. Virgin Islands, and Guam. (It also includes Canada.) Each entry lists the address and telephone number, and often the areas of practice and biographical information as well.

Don't assume that every lawyer in the country is listed here. The directory lists only those lawyers who chose to be listed.

The directory is quite flexible in that you can search in a number of ways. The easiest is to do a WAIS search for key terms, since this is a common search method at many sites on the Internet (see the sidebar *WAIS Searches* in my "Best Ways of Finding More and Better Sites" section at the end of Part Two). You can also search using West's *data fields*, which produces pretty much the same results as a key term search, just with different syntax. West provides a good and detailed explanation of data field searching if you are so inclined.

TAXES

There is, of course, no avoiding taxes. Fortunately, the sites in this section bring you everything from the tax forms themselves (straight from the IRS no less) to many different sources of tax advice from professionals.

Finding a Lawyer

I f you need a lawyer, there are a number of ways you can go about finding one. One way, of course, is the Internet. You'll find that a number of law firms have their own sites now, some of which are listed at

http://www.law.indiana.edu/law/lawfirms.html

You could also try West's Legal Directory of Lawyers and Law Firms, which I discuss nearby.

If you're more comfortable with direct human contact when seeking a professional reference, many county bar associations maintain lawyer referral services, which will be listed in your telephone book's yellow pages, probably under *Attorney Referral Services*, along with any others in your area.

Finally, there's no substitute for word of mouth. Ask your friends and colleagues if they've used an attorney they can recommend.

IRS Tax Forms and Information

http://www.ustreas.gov/treasury/bureaus/irs/irs.html

You can't file your returns electronically here, but at least you no longer have to go hunting madly around town looking for forms. This site contains all of the IRS tax forms and their accompanying instructions (Figure 2.10). With a few exceptions that are clearly identified, you can download the form you need, print it, fill it out, and file it when the time comes.

All forms and instructions are available in PCL (for Hewlett Packard printers), PDF (Adobe Acrobat), PS (for PostScript printers), and SGML formats, so most systems are covered. Forms in PDF format are searchable; for forms in any of the other formats, you must look down a list.

This site also provides answers to frequently asked questions about taxes, addresses for filing your return, and information about free tax assistance. If you must file a return, and just about everybody does, then this site is worth a visit.

Form **1040A** (99)	Department of the Treasury—Internal Revenue Service **U.S. Individual Income Tax Return**	**1994**	IRS Use Only—Do not write or staple in this space.

[Figure showing a 1040A tax form with fields for Label, filing status, and exemptions]

Label (See page 16.)
Use the IRS label. Otherwise, please print or type.

Your first name and initial | Last name | Your social security number
If a joint return, spouse's first name and initial | Last name | Spouse's social security number
Home address (number and street). If you have a P.O. box, see page 17. | Apt. no.
City, town or post office, state, and ZIP code If you have a foreign address, see page 17.

OMB No. 1545-0085

For Privacy Act and Paperwork Reduction Act Notice, see page 4.

Presidential Election Campaign Fund (See page 17.)
Do you want $3 to go to this fund? | Yes | No
If a joint return, does your spouse want $3 to go to this fund?

Note: Checking "Yes" will not change your tax or reduce your refund.

Check the box for your filing status (See page 17.)
Check only one box.
1 ☐ Single
2 ☐ Married filing joint return (even if only one had income)
3 ☐ Married filing separate return. Enter spouse's social security number above and full name here. ▶
4 ☐ Head of household (with qualifying person). (See page 18.) If the qualifying person is a child but not your dependent, enter this child's name here. ▶
5 ☐ Qualifying widow(er) with dependent child (year spouse died ▶ 19___). (See page 19.)

Figure your exemptions (See page 20.)
If more than seven dependents, see page 23.
6a ☐ Yourself. If your parent (or someone else) can claim you as a dependent on his or her tax return, do not check box 6a. But be sure to check the box on line 18b on page 2.
b ☐ Spouse
c Dependents:
(1) Name (first, initial, and last name) | (2) Check if under age 1 | (3) If age 1 or older, dependent's social security number | (4) Dependent's relationship to you | (5) No. of months lived in your home in 1994

No. of boxes checked on 6a and 6b ___
No. of your children on 6c who:
• lived with you ___
• did n't live with you due to divorce or separation (see page 23)

Figure 2.10:
Part of an onscreen 1040A form from the IRS Tax Forms and Information site

The Internal Revenue Code: U.S. Tax Law

http://www.tns.les.mit.edu/uscode/

This site contains a searchable, hypertext version of the Internal Revenue Code. The text of the code is broken down into its component sections, and you can jump to the one(s) you want via the links in the tables of contents provided or by using the built-in search program to search for key terms.

This site's usefulness as a reference, however, is limited by two important factors. First, as of this writing it is current only through October, 1993, so you must check it against a current, official version of the code to be certain that what you have is correct. Second, when you use the search program, it returns a series of links to sections that match the terms you searched for. These links don't describe or contain the title of the matching sections, though, so you won't know what you have until you've followed each one— a significant waste of time. If these two wrinkles could be ironed out, this would be an excellent site.

Taxing Times 1995

http://www.scubed.com:8001/tax/tax.html

This Web site is a public service of the S-Cubed division of Maxwell Labs. It contains a lot of information that was useful at the time for filing your 1994 tax returns, and links to other Internet tax sites. Hopefully, it will be updated for filing 1995 returns.

In addition to federal tax forms, you'll find links to tax forms for, at last count, five states and Canada. The site provides information on how to order forms by e-mail and how to get free tax assistance from the IRS. There are also links to other Internet tax sites. In short, if you do your own tax return, this is a good site to know about.

Tax Digest

http://www.unf.edu/misc/jmayer/taxdig.html

This page contains links to the last 13 issues of *Tax Digest*, a tax newsletter from Gary R. Hastings, a Dallas CPA; previous issues are also available. Each issue of the *Digest* covers quite a broad range of tax subjects, neatly summarized on the main page. If you like to keep abreast of tax developments, take a look here.

The author also distributes Tax Digest *by e-mail. There is a link on the page so that you can contact him easily.*

Tax World

http://omer.cba.neu.edu/home

Professor Thomas C. Omer of Northeastern University says he assembled this page to disseminate tax information on the Internet. This he has done quite well, but what is more, he has also made this page into a good teaching tool.

Professor Omer not only makes course syllabi and assignments available for his own tax courses, he has posted course descriptions and syllabi for all tax courses at Northeastern—a sensible use of computers in academia if there ever was one.

Visitors to his page who are looking for tax information will find links to other tax sites on the Internet, historical information about taxation, and a forum for discussing current tax issues. Comments about tax issues are invited and posted daily.

The Tax Prophet

http://www.taxprophet.com

This page, produced by San Francisco attorney Robert L. Sommers, contains a great deal of tax information. Visitors will find the full text of newspaper columns, newsletters, and scholarly articles written by Mr. Sommers on a wide variety of tax subjects, including tax planning, audits, and many many others.

Mr. Sommers also provides information and a detailed written analysis of current tax topics, such as, at the time of this writing, flat tax proposals.

The Villanova Tax Law Compendium

ming.law.vill.edu

The *Tax Law Compendium* is on a Gopher at Villanova University under the entry Villanova Tax Law Compendium. It is a collection of scholarly articles on a variety of tax law subjects that are written by Villanova faculty and law students. The full text of every article is available.

If you are using a Web browser you can go directly to the Compendium and do not have to step through the menus. Use the URL:

gopher://ming.law.vill.edu:70/11/.taxlaw/

The site is still fairly new. As of this writing, the number of articles available is small, but growing, and users can easily find articles of interest just by browsing the titles. When the number of titles increases, however, an index or summary file will be necessary.

The Bipartisan Congressional Commission on Entitlement and Tax Reform

http://www.charm.net:80/~dcarolco/

Appointed by President Clinton in 1993, the Commission is charged with making recommendations for "long-term changes to America's entitlement programs and tax structure." This Web page is a good exercise in making government information widely available.

Visitors to this page will find, among other things, the Commission's Interim Report to the President, detailing the problems involved in undertaking tax and entitlement reform and transcripts of testimony before the Commission. The transcripts are available for download. There is even a spreadsheet available for download that allows the user to see the fiscal implications of making changes to entitlement programs and taxes.

Public commentary is welcome.

If you want to run the Budget Shadow spreadsheet that is available from this site, you must have Lotus 1-2-3 for Windows. Also, be warned that the spreadsheet is a large file (approximately 2 Megabytes), so downloading it will take some time.

A MISCELLANY OF INTERESTING SITES

Inevitably when compiling a large list and then trying to organize it, there are a few items left over that aren't quite classifiable. Here are all the sites that don't easily slip into one of the previous sections but are of interest nonetheless.

Famous Supreme Court Cases: Barron v. Baltimore

John Marshall served as chief justice of the United States from 1801 to 1836 and presided over some of the most significant decisions in the nation's legal history. Although you can probably fill books about the significance of some of these early cases, like *Marbury v. Madison* and *Martin v. Hunter's Lessee*, discussed elsewhere in this book, I will include only one here.

Mr. Barron was the owner of a wharf in the Baltimore harbor, at which, he alleged, ships could no longer dock because of silt deposits caused by city street construction that diverted water flow. Barron sued the mayor and the city council of Baltimore for damages, alleging a violation of the Fifth Amendment's "takings" clause, which says: "nor shall private property be taken for public use, without just compensation."

Mr. Barron lost his case because, in 1833, the Bill of Rights applied only to the federal government and not to the states. Chief Justice Marshall wrote: "We are of the opinion that the ... fifth amendment [is] intended solely as a limitation on the exercise of power by the government of the United States, and is not applicable to legislation of the states."

Today, however, this is no longer true. Over the course of the twentieth century, the Supreme Court has ruled that most of the provisions of the first eight amendments in the Bill of Rights—including the "takings" clause—do apply to the states. This change occurred gradually, one provision and one case at a time (see, for example *Gideon v. Wainright,* presented elsewhere in this book). Why the change? What's the difference between *Barron v. Baltimore* in 1833 and today? The answer, in short, is the Fourteenth Amendment, for it is the guarantee of "due process" in the Fourteenth Amendment that applies the Bill of Rights to the states.

Banned Books On-Line

http://www.cs.cmu.edu/Web/People/spok/banned-books.html

Here you'll find the full text (not summaries) of books that have been banned at various times and places. It's an interesting assortment and includes *Huckleberry Finn, Fanny Hill,* Thomas Paine's *The Rights of*

Man, and *The Merchant of Venice* (see Figure 2.11). Perceived obscenity leads the list of reasons given for banning, but political motivations come a close second. Also available is a list of the most frequently challenged books in the USA, from the book *Banned in the U.S.A.*

Banned Books On-line

Welcome to this special exhibit of books that have been the objects of censorship or censorship attempts. The books featured here, ranging from *Ulysses* to *Little Red Riding Hood*, have been selected from the indexes on the On-line Books Page.

This page is a work in progress, and more works may be added to this page over time. Please inform spok@cs.cmu.edu of any new material that can be included here.

Books Suppressed or Censored by Legal Authorities

Ulysses by James Joyce was recently praised by CMU English professor and vice-provost Erwin Steinberg. (Steinberg also defended Carnegie Mellon's declaration to delete alt.sex and some 80 other newsgroups, claiming they were legally obligated to do so.) *Ulysses* was barred from the United States as obscene for 15 years, and was seized by U.S Postal Authorities in 1918 and 1930. The lifting of the ban in 1933 came only after advocates fought for the right to publish the book. (Please don't use this on-line copy if you are in the US, where it is still copyrighted.)

In 1930, U.S. Customs seized Harvard-bound copies of *Candide*, Voltaire's critically hailed satire, claiming obscenity. Two Harvard professors defended the work, and it was later admitted in a different edition. In 1944, the US Post Office demanded the omission of *Candide* from a mailed Concord Books catalog.

John Cleland's *Fanny Hill* (also known as *Memoirs of a Woman of Pleasure*) has been frequently suppressed since its initial publication in 1749. This story of a prostitute is known both for its frank sexual descriptions and its parodies of contemporary literature, such as Daniel Defoe's *Moll Flanders*.

Figure 2.11:
Banned Books On-line provides the full text of Ulysses, Candide, and Fanny Hill, among many others

---

Biomedical Ethics List

The Biomedical Ethics List can be subscribed to by sending a message to:

listserv@vm1.nodak.edu

Leave the subject line blank, and in the body of the message type the following:

subscribe biomed-l yourfirstname yourlastname

To unsubscribe, send a message to the same place (again, no subject line) saying

signoff biomed-l

An alternate address for subscribing is listserv@ndsuvm1.bitnet, *using the subscribe message above. Remember, though, if you use this address to subscribe, you must use it to unsubscribe as well, using the "signoff" message above.*

This mailing list will provide you with an ongoing discussion of ethical questions surrounding the burgeoning field of medical ethics. Issues raised include genetic screening, testing and therapy, fetal cell research, and euthanasia. Discussion is mostly among students and professionals in areas of medicine, law, and the social sciences. It's the kind of list where few questions are answered with finality but the subjects are invariably interesting.

Cornell Law Review

http://www.law.cornell.edu/clr/clr.htm

The *Cornell Law Review* is the main law journal published by the Cornell University Law School. Just about everything you'd want to know about it is available here, including the current editorial board and how to subscribe. Of more concrete use are the links to the full text of current issues of the review, including all articles and notes.

Law Talk

http://www.law.indiana.edu/law/lawtalk.html

With this service of the Indiana University School of Law, you can download sound files, each about a minute long, summarizing some aspect of civil or criminal law, expressed in layperson's language. Each file is written by a faculty member.

The files are about half a megabyte each and can be saved to your hard drive to be played later. To play the files you'll need a sound device (such as a sound card) and a program capable of loading .AU (basic audio) files. Web browsers such as Netscape and the Internet Explorer include a sound player. Figure 2.12 shows a sound file explaining double jeopardy being played by the Internet Explorer.

Figure 2.12:
Sound files explaining legal concepts can be downloaded from the Law Talk page.

The Legal Domain Network

http://www.kentlaw.edu/lawnet/lawnet.html

This home page provides a jumping-off point to an assortment of mailing lists and Usenet news groups. The lists include a dozen or more legal discussion groups, another dozen on political subjects, and some miscellany on intellectual property rights, taxes, guns, and drugs. Something for everybody!

Legal and Ethical Internet Resources

http://www.nau.edu/legal.html

A source for administrators of Internet sites. Questions of content, disclaimers, and how to formulate acceptable use statements. Warning screens and how to use them are also covered.

The university or other Internet administrator having to deal with liability and other legal issues will find lots to chew on here.

A Legal Newsgroup

misc.legal

Misc.legal is wide-ranging news group with content that varies from intelligent discussion to toxic flames. The subject matter is very freewheeling and is unfettered by a moderator. You might also want to check out misc.legal.moderated where discussions are curtailed once they degenerate into *ad hominem* attacks.

Sex Laws

http://www.cc.gatech.edu/grads/g/Mark.Gray/Sex__Laws.html

This is a promising but as yet undeveloped Web page that plans to cover the laws defining what sexual acts are criminal in various states. As of this writing, only Georgia and Kansas were covered in detail, though there are hypertext links to the California and Florida penal codes.

BEST "SMORGASBOARD SITES": SITES WITH EVERYTHING!

Each of the sites in this section offers a lot of good and varied legal information, and many of them aim to be *overall* resources to the topic of law in general. These sites contain (or contain links to) some of the best legal information available on the Internet.

A few of the sites here call themselves "libraries," which I think is an appropriate metaphor. As with libraries, you can go to these sites to look for something specific or you can spend an entire afternoon just browsing (I'm not exaggerating—I've done it). If you do spend time looking around, don't be surprised if you see links to the same sites popping up over and over again in different places. The frequency of such "repeats" is usually an indication of how good those sites are, in that they have been judged worthy of inclusion by a number of site organizers.

The folks who put these resources together have organized them in a number of ways, so it will pay you to look around, decide which ones interest you and which ones you're most comfortable with, and add them to your list of sites to return to frequently. There's something here for everyone.

Famous Supreme Court Cases: Cohen v. California

This is one of my favorite First Amendment "freedom of speech" cases. In April 1968, Paul Cohen was arrested for disturbing the peace in the hallway of the Los Angeles County courthouse. He was convicted and sentenced to 30 days in jail. His crime? He was not being noisy, disruptive, or violent. All he did was wear a T-shirt that said "F*** the Draft."

Mr. Cohen appealed and his case reached the U.S. Supreme Court, which overturned his conviction. The state cannot, the Court said, punish someone for the content of his speech, even if it is immature, disagreeable, and offensive. Or, as Justice Harlan wrote for the Court: "Surely the State has no right to cleanse public debate to the point where it is grammatically palatable to the most squeamish among us."

Indeed, this case contains truly fine writing about the importance of freedom of speech: "To many, the immediate consequence of this freedom may often appear to be only verbal tumult, discord, and even offensive utterance. These are, however, within established limits, in truth necessary side effects of the broader enduring values which the process of open debate permits us to achieve. That the air may at times seem filled with verbal cacophony is, in this sense not a sign of weakness but of strength. We cannot lose sight of the fact that, in what otherwise might seem a trifling and annoying instance of individual distateful abuse of a privilege, these fundamental societal values are truly implicated... "

Yahoo on Law

http://www.yahoo.com/Law

Yahoo is an Internet subject index from Stanford University; this page is the index to law on the Internet. It gives you a list of subject links in the general area of law, from Antitrust to Usenet, which take you to links for sites strong in those subjects (Figure 2.13).

Law
• **Antitrust** *(2)*
• **Arbitration and Mediation** *(3)* [new]
• **Cases** *(23)*
• **Commercial** *(4)*
• **Consumer** *(4)*
• **Countries** *(28)*
• **Crime@** *(32)* [new]
• **Environmental@** *(3)*
• **Family Law** *(2)*
• **General Information** *(10)*
• **Human Rights@** *(20)* [new]
• **Immigration** *(17)*
• **Institutes** *(11)*
• **Intellectual Property** *(53)* [new]
• **International** *(6)*
• **Journals** *(11)*
• **Judicial Branch@** *(8)*
• **Law Firms and Legal Agencies@** *(118)* [new]
• **Law Schools** *(48)*
• **Law Software Companies@** *(3)*

Figure 2.13:
Some of the legal sub-
jects on the Yahoo
WWW page

If you are looking for law-related information on subjects that you can't find elsewhere in my "Have a Problem? Check Here First" section, go directly to Yahoo to find what you need.

Law Summaries

http://www.law.cornell.edu:80/topics/topic2.html

This site isn't quite like anything else I've seen on the Internet, and it's a knockout. It provides a short summary of, and bibliography for, many different topics in the law. If you need a short explanation of a subject and also want to know where to go to get further information about it, I recommend checking here.

The main page has a long list of links for different legal subjects. Each link takes you to a three-to-four-paragraph summary of the subject, and the summary contains links to the text of any laws or regulations discussed. After the summary comes a list of links to sites with related laws and material. These can be, for example, court decisions or treaties and conventions. And as if this weren't enough, books on the subject are also mentioned. The only disappointment was that the project is not yet complete; the entries for some topics have not yet been written.

The Legal Researcher's Internet Toolkit

http://www.law.indiana.edu/lawlib/toolkit2.html

This site is a good place to start looking if you want to browse. It's also good if you're looking for something in a particular subject area but don't know the exact name of the document or organization you need. Although this page will not by any means take you to every law-related site on the Internet, it does point in a number of possibly useful directions.

The page you start with here is a short one, with only a few links. These are essentially general topic headings, such as "International Law," "State Law," or "Finding People," which can take you to further links, which may in turn take you to additional links before you arrive at specific sites of the kind described.

If you are looking for something specific and don't have the time or inclination to go casting about in cyberspace on the trail of someone else's idea of what belongs under what general topic heading, you should consider using a "search program"—a tool that enables you to search a huge portion of the Web or Gopherspace by subject, or even for a particular word or combination of words. See my "Best Ways of Finding More and Better Sites" section at the end of Part Two.

The House of Representatives Internet Law Library

http://www.pls.com:8001/

Like the Legal Researcher's Internet Toolkit in the previous entry, the House of Representatives Internet Law Library is also a short Web page with only a few links, which serve as general topic headings, such as U.S. State and Territorial Laws and Treaties and International Law (Figure 2.14) Clicking on these links takes you to other links or to specific sites.

The stated purpose of the Library is "to provide easy access to the law-related resources of the Internet." It does indeed do this, pointing you to over 1600 different sites. On the one hand, if you're looking for something specific, wading through that much data can be a hindrance, because the document you want to read or institution you want to contact could be buried

Figure 2.14:
The Internet Law
Library from the House
of Representatives

The U.S. House of Representatives Internet Law Library

Welcome!

- about this directory
- U.S. Federal laws (arranged by original published source)
- U.S. Federal laws (arranged by agency)
- U.S. state and territorial laws
- Laws of other nations
- Treaties and international law
- Laws of all jurisdictions (arranged by subject)
- Law school law library catalogues and services
- Attorney and legal profession directories
- Reviews of law books

Your Comments Please!
    Let us know if you have any comments about the presentation of this information, or any ideas or concerns you want to convey to the House of Representatives. (usc@hr.house.gov)

many levels deep in the links. On the other hand, if your purpose is to browse or to get the lay of the land, as it were, then this much information will appeal to you. If you are looking for information on government, U.S. law, or state law, this site is strong in these areas and this is a good place to start.

The Legal Information Institute

http://www.law.cornell.edu/

The Legal Information Institute (LII) is part of the Cornell University School of Law, and its Web page is one of the best law-related sites on the Internet. The page is divided into roughly four sections, with the first one, "Items of Special Current Interest," receiving the emphasis. This section contains a list of links to legal sites that are new on the Net (Figure 2.15). If you want to keep abreast of what is available out there, you should check in with the LII regularly.

Don't ignore the other three sections, which contain information about the LII, links to legal material organized by topic and source, and links to other Internet sites devoted to law.

In addition to providing access to a lot of good legal information, the LII has also written its own Web browser, called Cello. Cello is available here for download, along with a range of support information, including a list of

Items of Special Current Interest Available via the LII Server Include:
• **An LII Focus on:**
☐ Impact of Information Technology on Law
☐ A New Court Statistics Service
☐ "Weaving Neighborhoods" - Article at internetMCI
☐ Court Rules (Including the Supreme Court's Proposed New Rules and the Federal Rules of Evidence)
☐ Lawyers on the Internet
☐ Internet Access to the Work of Congress
• Documents on the Proposed Miscrosoft Antitrust Settlement, Including Judge Sporkin's Feb. 14 Opinion:
☐ From the PC Magazine WWW Server
☐ From the Justice Dept. Gopher: Judge Sporkin's Opinion and the Appeal
• Wisconsin Citation Reform Proposal **(Hearing in March 1995)**
• ABA Draft Standards for Accreditation of Law Libraries
• National Information Infrastructure Report
• Public Information on the National Information Infrastructure - H. Perrit
• Full United States Code **[LII/New on Net]**
• Directory of U.S. High Courts **[LII/New on Net]**
• Alaska Decisions - Alaska Supreme Court & Court of Appeals **[New on Net]**
• Draft New Uniform and Model Laws from the National Conference of Commissioners on Uniform State Laws **[New on Net]**
• Copyright Clearance Center **[Net on Net]**
• National Center for State Courts WWW Site **[New on Net]**

Figure 2.15:
Some Items of Special
Current Interest

hardware and software requirements, answers to frequently asked questions, and a searchable database of messages from *CELLO-L*, a list mailing devoted to using and discussing Cello.

If you don't have a Web browser and can't get to the LII home page, Cello is available without charge by Anonymous FTP from the address

ftp.law.cornell.edu

in the /pub/LII/Cello directory. The file name is cello.zip.

The WWW Virtual Library: Law

http://www.law.indiana.edu:80/law/lawindex.html

The bulk of this Web page contains a long, descriptive, alphabetical list of law-related sites, beginning with the ACLU Free Reading Room and taking you all the way through the WHO Gopher (the Gopher for the World Health Organization).

Like any other site in this section, you can spend a long time browsing here, if that's what you're after, but the main strength of the page is this alphabetical list. To give you some small idea of what's available, there are links that take you to sites devoted to specific areas of the law (e.g., advertising law, Irish law), links to primary law sources (e.g., the Uniform Code of

Military Justice), sites with information about government organizations (e.g., the federal government or United Nations), and even links to law schools and libraries. If you need to find something in a particular subject area but don't know the exact name of the document or organization you need, this list is a good place to start looking.

The Rice University Government Gopher

riceinfo.rice.edu

This Texas-sized collection (the menu alone is about 100,000 bytes) is located on a Gopher at Rice University in Houston under the menu entries Information by Subject Area and Government, Political Science, and Law (see Figure 2.16).

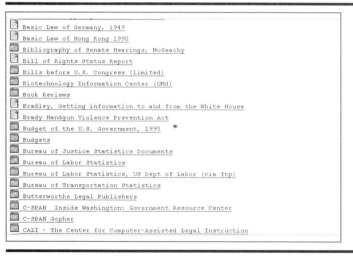

Figure 2.16:
Just some of the Information available from the Rice University Government Gopher

```
Basic Law of Germany, 1949
Basic Law of Hong Kong 1990
Bibliography of Senate Hearings, McGeachy
Bill of Rights Status Report
Bills before U.S. Congress (limited)
Biotechnology Information Center (UMd)
Book Reviews
Bradley, Getting information to and from the White House
Brady Handgun Violence Prevention Act
Budget of the U.S. Government, 1995
Budgets
Bureau of Justice Statistics Documents
Bureau of Labor Statistics
Bureau of Labor Statistics, US Dept of Labor (via ftp)
Bureau of Transportation Statistics
Butterworths Legal Publishers
C-SPAN  Inside Washington: Government Resource Center
C-SPAN Gopher
CALI - The Center for Computer-Assisted Legal Instruction
```

If you are using a Web browser you do not have to step through the Gopher menus; you can go directly to the collection. Use the URL:

gopher://riceinfo.rice.edu/11/Subject/Government

This site is particularly strong in the area of government. In fact, there is so much available here that it isn't possible in this small space to give a clear picture of all the things you'll find. Suffice it to say that not only will you find information widely referenced elsewhere on the Net—the Congressional Record, for example—but you will also find some real gems that are rarely referenced anywhere else, such as information from the Johnson Presidential Library.

This site is a real treasure trove; if you need to browse a particular topic in the area of government, this is an excellent place to start looking.

LAWLinks

http://www.counsel.com/cchome.html

LAWLinks is a public-access Web page from Lexis Counsel Connect, a subscription service for lawyers to exchange e-mail and information. There is a good-sized collection of material here, including links to other law-related collections and links to federal and state government information. A directory of lawyers and law firms is also advertised, though as of this writing it is not yet on line.

The best feature of this page, however, is its topical law index, an alphabetical series of subject links from Administrative Law to Women and the Law. Each link takes you to a group of additional links. There are more links and better information for some subjects than others, but as legal information on the Internet is ever expanding, this is only to be expected.

If you are looking for information about a particular kind of law or legal subject, starting on this page is a good idea.

WooNet

http://www.mcs.com/~carolwoo/home.html

Carol Woodbury describes herself as a "freelance writer on law and technology topics." She's also a former lawyer and programmer. I like her Web page, not only because of its utility, but also because it shows what a person of energy, intelligence, and good humor can accomplish.

You'll get the best legal action here by following the Areas of Law link. This brings you to an alphabetical list of subject links, from Advertising to White Collar Crime, which in turn take you to links about the named subject. These links are almost all for law firms that practice in the area in question, and their sites are a mixed bag. The more useful sites provide information about the subject and/or links to other legal information on the Internet. Others merely give information about the firm.

In addition to finding this page entertaining, you may find it of value if you are looking for information about a particular area of the law.

A List of Legal Lists

http://tarlton.law.utexas.edu/library/netref/listserv/lawlists.html

This is a list of about a hundred list mailings on the topic of law and legal issues, put together by the Tarlton Law Library at the University of Texas at Austin School of Law. Each mailing on this list is described briefly and instructions for subscribing are given (see Figure 2.17).

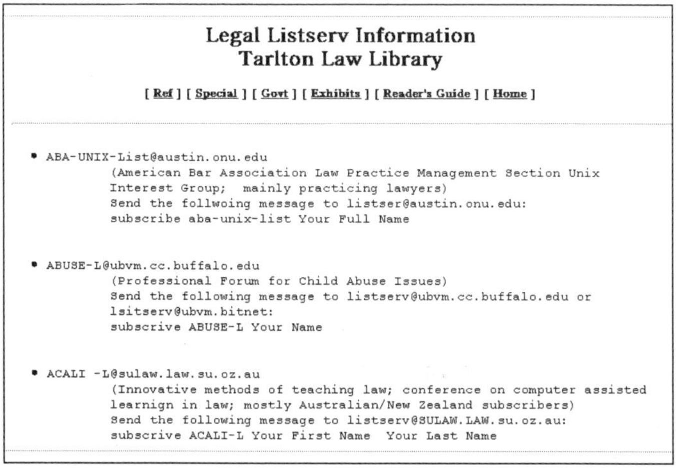

Legal Listserv Information
Tarlton Law Library

[**Ref**] [**Special**] [**Govt**] [**Exhibits**] [**Reader's Guide**] [**Home**]

- ABA-UNIX-List@austin.onu.edu
      (American Bar Association Law Practice Management Section Unix
      Interest Group; mainly practicing lawyers)
      Send the follwoing message to listser@austin.onu.edu:
      subscribe aba-unix-list Your Full Name

- ABUSE-L@ubvm.cc.buffalo.edu
      (Professional Forum for Child Abuse Issues)
      Send the following message to listserv@ubvm.cc.buffalo.edu or
      lsitserv@ubvm.bitnet:
      subscribe ABUSE-L Your Name

- ACALI -L@sulaw.law.su.oz.au
      (Innovative methods of teaching law; conference on computer assisted
      learnign in law; mostly Australian/New Zealand subscribers)
      Send the following message to listserv@SULAW.LAW.su.oz.au:
      subscribe ACALI-L Your First Name Your Last Name

Figure 2.17:
The beginning of the
Tarlton Law Library list
of approximately one
hundred list mailings

The subjects represented in the list are diverse. Some are quite broad, others are quite narrow. Some are geared to particular participants (administrative law professors and lecturers, for example) and others are more general. If you enjoy the kind of interaction and exchange that list participation provides, there is probably a mail list here for you.

Legal Lists, Newsgroups, FTP Sites, and Library Catalogs

dewey.lib.ncsu.edu

This list is located on a North Carolina State University Libraries Gopher under the following sequence of menu entries: NCSU's "Library Without Walls", then Reference Desk, then Guides..., and finally List of law related Internet resources, Jensen, in that order.

If you are using a Web browser you do not have to step through the Gopher menus; you can go directly to the list. Use the URL:

gopher://dewey.lib.ncsu.edu:70/00/library/reference/guides/jensen

The list details legal mail lists, law library catalogs, FTP sites, and newsgroups about law, politics, government, and librarianship. Subscription information (for mail lists), file location (for FTP sites), and login information (for library catalogs) is provided. Given the breadth of topics covered here, you will probably find some of the entries a bit far afield from your interests. Nevertheless, if you're looking for legal information in one or more of these forms, take a look here and you may come away with an idea of which resources best suit your needs.

Online Law Journals and Periodicals

http://www.usc.edu/dept/law-lib/legallst/journals.html

With the explosion of legal information on line, law journals are beginning to appear on the Internet. Most law schools publish one or more law journals. These are academic publications, and are often devoted to a particular legal topic. Some of the oldest and most prestigous are "umbrella" journals, which means they publish about all legal topics.

The full text of some of the journals is available on line, while others publish only abstracts of their articles and ask you to purchase the issues that interest you. This Web page, from the University of Southern California Law Library, is a complete list of law journals that are on line, with links to each.

Famous Supreme Court Cases: Miranda v. Arizona

"You have the right to remain silent. Anything you say can and will be used against you in a court of law. You have the right to consult with an attorney. If you cannot afford one, an attorney will be appointed for you." These words, or ones much like them, are known to viewers of American police shows as *Miranda warnings*, given when the police are "Mirandizing" a suspect.

The case known as *Miranda v. Arizona* (1963) was actually four consolidated cases. (The Supreme Court will consolidate cases and decide them together when they present the same legal issues.) In each case, a suspect in custody was interrogated by the police or prosecuting attorney without being made aware of his constitutional rights. In each case, the suspect made a confession that was used at trial. In each case, the suspect was convicted.

The Supreme Court overturned three of the four convictions because the suspects' statements to the authorities "were obtained under circumstances that did not meet constitutional standards for protection of the privilege against self-incrimination," which is guaranteed by the Fifth Amendment. Chief Justice Earl Warren wrote that "[i]n order to … permit a full opportunity to exercise the privilege against self-incrimination, the accused must be adequately and effectively apprised of his rights and the exercise of those rights must be fully honored." To make suspects aware of their right against self-incrimination, the chief justice set out in his opinion what came to be known as the Miranda warnings.

The Lawyer's Desk Reference

The entries in this section contain information that lawyers will often have in their offices and libraries, such as court decisions, the Federal Rules of Civil Procedure, or a handbook of legal citation. I think, therefore, that as a practical matter lawyers may find the entries here more useful than non-lawyers will. That said, lawyers should be aware that, with the exception of the U.S. Supreme Court decisions from 1993 on, none of the court decisions, codes, or rules here are official. These sources are most useful as quick references and not as research tools.

COURTS AND COURT DECISIONS

More and more court decisions are making their way onto the Internet. You'll find decisions of a number of federal courts at the sites in this section. Some state court decisions are available at sites in my "State Law on the Internet" section later in Part Two.

U.S. SUPREME COURT

Just about every lawyer will have a shelf full of Supreme Court decisions. However, the online versions are easier to search to find what you want.

U.S. Supreme Court Decisions

http://www.law.cornell.edu/supct/supct.table.html

Since 1990, the United States Supreme Court has published its opinions electronically. They are available here. For each case, you will find a syllabus of the Court's holding, the Court's published opinion, and any concurring or dissenting opinions written. You can find cases you want by searching for key terms or through the comprehensive topic index, in which you will find everything the Court has dealt with, from *abortion* through *workers' compensation*. Also, cases in the current term are listed by date; cases from prior terms are listed by the names of the parties.

Nonlawyers may find the Court's opinions a bit obscure; it can be difficult to see the practical, not to mention the political, consequences of a case amid the many pages of legal issues, legal terminology, and citations (see Figure 2.18).

```
SUPREME COURT OF THE UNITED STATES
--------
Nos. 93-1456 and 93-1828
--------
U. S. TERM LIMITS, INC., et al., PETITIONERS
93-1456                    v.
RAY THORNTON et al.

WINSTON BRYANT, ATTORNEY GENERAL OF
ARKANSAS, PETITIONER
93-1828                    v.
BOBBIE E. HILL et al.
on writs of certiorari to the supreme court of
arkansas
[May 22, 1995]

    Justice Stevens delivered the opinion of the Court.
    The Constitution sets forth qualifications for member-
ship in the Congress of the United States.  Article I, 2,
cl. 2, which applies to the House of Representatives,
provides:
        -No Person shall be a Representative who shall
not have attained to the Age of twenty five Years,
and been seven Years a Citizen of the United
States, and who shall not, when elected, be an
```

Figure 2.18:
The beginning of a recent Supreme Court opinion holding state term limit laws unconstitutional

Lawyers should note that these opinions are official for cases handed down beginning in 1993, subject to any corrections made in the U.S. Reports.

The Hermes Project

The electronic opinions issued by the Supreme Court are archived and made available by Case Western Reserve University's Hermes Project. The Project has an FTP site at the address:

ftp.cwru.edu

and the opinions are located in the /hermes directory.

Current opinions are available to download in a number of formats: Atex8000 in the /atex directory (this is the format used by the Court), ASCII in the /ascii directory, and WordPerfect 5.1 in the /word-perfect directory.

I found the file naming convention difficult but it makes a certain kind of sense once you get used to it. All of the file names begin with the Court's docket number, so you must determine this first. (You can get it from the Index file or from the Supreme Court site discussed above.) After the docket number in the file name comes an extension with an identifying letter in it. This extension tells you what kind of opinion is in the file. Here are the identifying letters:

O opinion of the Court

C concurring opinion

D dissenting opinion

S case syllabus

Once you have this figured out you should be able to download the files you want.

Attorneys should also note that Hermes has the plaintiffs' and respondents' briefs filed for some, but not all cases. These too are organized by docket number in the directory /hermes/briefs/zip-archives. The briefs are not text files, though; the original briefs have been scanned in. What you get are a bunch of graphics files in .TIF format, put into a .ZIP archive that, for reasons I don't understand, have the extension .ZPT. Be aware that these files are quite large, usually about 1.5 megabytes, and can take a long time to download. The briefs may be a useful resource to you, but you'll have to do some work to get what you want.

FEDERAL APPELLATE COURTS

Below the U.S. Supreme Court are the 13 federal appeals courts, which are also called Circuit courts. Two of the Circuit courts, the Third and Eleventh Circuits, have made their decisions available on the Internet.

Decisions of the Third Circuit Court of Appeals

http://ming.law.vill.edu/Fed-Ct/ca03.html

The federal Courts of Appeals or Circuit Courts are for the most part organized geographically. The Third Circuit hears appeals in cases coming from:

Delaware

New Jersey

Pennsylvania

U.S. Virgin Islands

Recent Third Circuit decisions (currently they begin with cases decided in 1994) are available to read and to download at this site from the Villanova Center for Information Law and Policy.

It is not difficult to find a case that you are looking for—you can search all cases for key words. Additionally, if you know when the case was decided, you can look on the chronological case list.

The main reason I like this site, though, is that it includes a feature I've not seen before. Not only are the cases available for download in ASCII, Word, and WordPerfect formats, but if you are in the 215 or 610 area codes, you can fax the case directly to your fax number.

Lawyers should note that the cases are not official and there are no annotations. Therefore they are best used for reference and not for research.

Decisions of the Eleventh Circuit Court of Appeals

http://www.law.emory.edu/11circuit/index.html

The federal Courts of Appeals or Circuit Courts are for the most part organized geographically. The Eleventh Circuit hears appeals in cases coming from the following states:

....
Alabama
....
Florida
....
Georgia

Recent Eleventh Circuit decisions (currently they begin with cases decided in November 1994) are available to read and to download at this Emory University site.

Cases are not hard to find—there is a built-in search program that you can use to search all cases for key terms. Additionally, you can look in a list of cases arranged chronologically or a list arranged by the names of the parties.

Cases are available for download as .RTF files (Rich Text Format), which pretty much any word processor can read these days.

Famous Supreme Court Cases: Gideon v. Wainright

This 1963 case is one of the more famous Supreme Court cases. It is the subject of *Gideon's Trumpet*, a book by *New York Times* writer Anthony Lewis, later made into a TV movie starring Henry Fonda.

Mr. Gideon was tried and convicted in Florida of breaking and entering into a pool hall. He appeared at his trial with no attorney and no money to hire one. When he asked the trial judge to appoint an attorney for him, the judge refused, saying (correctly) that Florida law at the time only permitted court-appointed lawyers for indigent defendants charged with capital crimes (i.e., crimes for which you could get the death penalty). Gideon was left to defend himself and though he did a credible job for someone with no legal training, he was convicted.

The Sixth Amendment to the Constitution provides "In all criminal prosecutions, the accused shall enjoy the right ... to have the Assistance of Counsel for his defence." Since 1938 this has meant in federal courts that an attorney must be appointed for indigent defendants. Gideon, however, was tried in Florida state court, where different rules applied. He argued in a habeas corpus petition to the Supreme Court that his conviction violated this Sixth Amendment right. The Supreme Court agreed, held that the Sixth Amendment right to counsel should apply to state courts as well as federal courts, and overturned Gideon's conviction. Ever since this case, indigent defendants in both state and federal courts can have lawyers appointed for them.

Oh, and Gideon? On retrial, with a defense attorney this time, he was acquitted.

LAWS, CODES, AND RULES

In this section you'll find unofficial copies of the United States Code and the Code of Federal Regulations here, along with some of the Federal Rules, and even a citation guide. More and more state laws are available on the Internet as well and you'll find these in my "State Law on the Internet" section later in Part Two.

The United States Code

http://www.law.cornell.edu/uscode/

This site has the entire text of the United States Code—all federal laws—a handy thing to have on your desktop considering that the code takes up a number of shelves in a library.

Attorneys should be aware that this code is not official and does not have annotations. It is best used for reference and not research.

Finding what you are looking for in the code here is not difficult. If you are looking for a common or well-known statute (the Americans with Disabilities Act, for example), you will probably find a link to it in the Table of Popular Names, which is an alphabetical list of acts and laws just under 400,000 bytes long.

You can also search for key terms, provided you know which Title (i.e., volume) contains what you're looking for—you can't (yet) search the entire code all at once. On the main page there is a list of links to each of the 50 Titles that make up the code, and the links describe the contents of each Title (Figure 2.19).

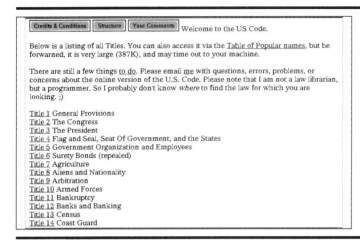

Figure 2.19:
The main page of the
United States Code
from the Legal
Information Institute
at Cornell University.
The figure shows the
first 14 of the 50 Titles
in the code.

The Code of Federal Regulations (CFR)

http://www.pls.com:8001/his/cfr.html

The Code of Federal Regulations contains all of the regulations issued by executive branch departments and agencies. Anyone who uses it regularly knows that it is an ungainly bear of a collection. It's huge—occupying shelf upon shelf in the library—and poorly indexed. This site, part of the House of Representatives Internet Law Library can be a boon to anyone who needs to work with the CFR.

Attorneys should note that the CFR here is not official and you should check what you find against the official, printed version. A warning at the site suggests the same.

The entire CFR is available here and you can access it with a powerful search program. With it you can search for key terms (using the Search option) or you can do what is called a "Concept Search," where all you have to do is enter a short description of what you are looking for. There are even "Advisors," which will suggest additional search terms to you. The search program is very difficult to use, however. It will take some trial and error and you should read the available help.

The Federal Rules of Civil Procedure (FRCP)

http://www.law.cornell.edu/rules/frcp/overview.htm

The Federal Rules of Civil Procedure are the rules that govern civil actions in the federal district (trial) courts. They are of use primarily to attorneys who practice in the federal courts and to first-year law students taking Civil Procedure.

Attorneys should use this site for reference only. The Rules here are neither official nor annotated.

You'll find links to the Rules in numerical order. It would have been nice for the layperson, though, if there were a search function. Fortunately, references within the text of a Rule to other Rules appear as hypertext links, which is a convenience.

The Federal Rules of Evidence

http://www.law.cornell.edu/rules/fre/overview.html

The Federal Rules of Evidence are the rules that govern the admission of evidence at trials in federal court. They are of use primarily to attorneys who practice in the federal courts and to law students studying Evidence.

Attorneys should use this site for reference only. The Rules here are neither official nor annotated.

You'll find on the page links to the Rules in numerical order which is appropriate since the Rules are known by and used by number. References within the text of a Rule to other Rules appear as hypertext links, which is a convenience, as is the availability of WAIS searches for key terms. (With the WAIS search capability, you can search for any word or words you like, and the built-in search program will respond with a list of links to the sections that contain what you searched for. For more information on how to compose WAIS searches, see the sidebar *WAIS Searches* in my "Best Ways of Finding More and Better Sites" section at the end of Part Two).

The Rules of Professional Conduct

http://www.law.cornell.edu:80/lawyers/ruletable.html

The Rules of Professional Conduct govern attorneys' actions toward their clients, other attorneys, the courts and tribunals they practice before, and the public in general. This site offers a copy of the Idaho Rules as being representative of the Rules in most states. Note, though, that although the Rules are quite similar from state to state, there can be important differences between states. If you have a question about attorney conduct, you should check a local law library for the Rules in your state.

Legal Citation

http://www.law.cornell.edu:80/citation/citation.table.html

Like any other discipline that involves research and writing, law has developed a system for citing sources and authorities. The benefits of a uniform system are obvious: it allows anyone—a judge reading a motion or brief submitted to the court, an attorney reading a case, a researcher reading a law review article—to find and read the case, statute, article, or book referred to in the writing.

This Web page provides an explanation of the system of legal citation. The introduction to the system is suitable for nonlawyers, and shows what to cite and how to cite it. Lawyers will find the page to be a handy reference for those times when they can't find their Blue Book (see the sidebar nearby called *How to Read a Case Citation*). There is a link on this page to an explanation, with examples, of each kind of citation you are likely to need. I found it best to jump right to the examples, though, because the explanations aren't as clearly set out as they could be.

COMMERCIAL SERVICES FOR LAWYERS

This section contains sites that offer or give information about commercial electronic legal services, like the large and well-known legal research services LEXIS-NEXIS and Westlaw.

How to Read a Case Citation

L et's take an example: *Loving v. Virginia, 388 U.S. 1 (1967)*, a famous U.S. Supreme Court case holding anti-miscegenation laws unconstitutional. There are three easy pieces in a citation. The first piece, *Loving v. Virginia*, is the name of the case, made up of the names of the parties, separated by *v.* for "versus." The middle piece I'll get to in the next paragraph. The last piece, *(1967)* in this example, is simply the date the court handed down its decision in the case.

The middle piece, *388 U.S. 1* in this example, is where the action is. Court decisions are found in a series of volumes called "Reports" or "Reporters," in which all the decisions of a court (or a group of courts) are printed. The abbreviation *U.S.* that you see in the example is for the *United States Reports*, which is where the Supreme Court decisions are printed. These reports take up a good part of a wall in a law library. The number preceding it is the volume number, and the number after it is the page number. All you have to do to find the *Loving* case, then, is pull out volume 388 of the *United States Reports* and turn to page 1. Simple, once you know how to do it.

To find cases from other courts, you'll need to know the name and abbreviation of the proper Reports. Since each court in the country has its own set of reports, each with its own name and abbreviation, I can't list them all here, but you can ask the reference librarian at a law library or ask for "the Blue Book": *A Uniform System of Citation* (Cambridge: Harvard Law Review Association, 1991).

LEXIS-NEXIS Communication Center

http://www.lexis-nexis.com/

LEXIS-NEXIS is a large, commercial "legal, news, and business information" service. This Internet site is primarily intended for subscribers or those who are interested in subscribing.

If you want to know more about LEXIS-NEXIS and haven't already taken the plunge, look to this site for information about the service, for bulletins and newsletters, and for answers to frequently asked questions. If you are already a subscriber, look to this site for a command reference and list of libraries, and a Telnet link that lets you connect via the Internet.

The Seamless WEBsite™

http://seamless.com

Now here is someone with a really good idea who has, I think, gotten in on the ground floor.

If you're an attorney or legal service provider and like the idea of having a presence on the Internet, but don't have the time or know-how to get it done, take a look here. The Seamless WEBsite will design and maintain pages on the World Wide Web for you. A number of different plans at different prices are available.

Once you get on the Internet, you'll find some other useful features on the WEBsite as well. If you need or are offering legal work or services, you can post a message detailing what you need or have. There is a forum for the exchange of ideas and for posting articles on law or computers. There are also, as you would expect, Web pages for attorneys and law firms, as well as links to other law-related sites on the Internet.

West Publishing Internet Information Center

http://www.westpub.com

Westlaw, from West Publishing Co., is an electronic legal research service (and competitor of LEXIS-NEXIS, above). This Internet site provides information for both current and prospective Westlaw subscribers. At this site you will find a description of all of the different Westlaw services available and also a link to West's Legal Directory of Lawyers and Law Firms. (See the entry for this above).

MISCELLANEOUS

The sites in this section don't fit neatly into any of the other sections but still may be of interest to lawyer and nonlawyer both.

The Global Arbitration Mediation Association, Inc.

http://www.gama.com

This association is a private provider of arbitration and mediation services, an area commonly referred to as *ADR*, for *alternative dispute resolution*. Its Web page, aside from advertising its services, contains some helpful information.

If you're interested in ADR you will find here a long description of arbitration and how it works, which can be interesting even to nonlawyers. If you're a lawyer you will appreciate the fifty or so forms collected in a forms bank to add to your own boilerplate and forms collections. The forms cover a number of different subjects, including arbitration (naturally), contracts, real estate, corporations, and business agreements.

LawMall™

http://www.ocsny.com:80/lawmall

This is an information clearinghouse and reference site with a grab bag of stuff for "lawyers, clients, and legal service providers." You will find here articles by attorneys on various current legal issues, and lawyers will find this site to be a place to advertise, even to post your résumé. It's a very changeable site, so check it out frequently. When I last checked, I found something that even nonlawyers might find useful—electronic correspondence courses. These are taught by e-mail, apparently, and cover a number of subjects.

Much of the LawMall is unfinished at the time of this writing, but some of the planned features look promising. In the future the site is slated to have a law dictionary on line, as well as biographies of state and federal judges, complete with judges' individual rules.

Checking Out Law Schools and Law Libraries

Whether you're thinking of becoming a lawyer or already know your way around the profession, you'll find some of the best legal stuff to be found in this section, which highlights law schools and law libraries on the Internet. Not only will you find information on how to get into law school, there are sites here for law school professors as well. You'll also find schools and libraries that have established a presence on the Net, and some outstanding individual sites.

INFORMATION FOR PROSPECTIVE LAW STUDENTS

Thinking about going to law school? In addition to collecting applications from schools you'd like to attend, you'll need to take the LSAT test. You'll find LSAT information on the first site in this section.

The Law School Admission Council

http://www.lsac.org

If you're planning to apply to law school, take a look at this site. It tells you when the LSATs are offered and how much they cost. If you have a Web browser (such as Netscape or Mosaic) that supports online forms, you can order LSAT and LSAT registration information here. There is no cost. While you're at it, you can also order practice exams that are actual past LSAT exams ($6 each or $14 for three, plus postage and handling), and financial aid information (no cost).

The Princeton Review Admissions Wizard

http://www.review.com/law/2000.html

If you think you *might* like to go to law school, but you haven't decided whether to apply or where you might like to go, take a look at the Admissions Wizard from the Princeton Review, a prominent company in standardized test preparation.

First and foremost, you'll find a searchable database of law school reviews. You can get information about any number of law schools by searching for the name of the school, the name of a state, or even a region of the country (e.g., "north-east" or "south-west"). There are also tips on how the admissions process works, whom you should ask for letters of recommendation, how you should deal with writing the personal statement required in every application, the cost of going to law school, and financial aid.

LAW SCHOOLS ON THE INTERNET

If you're looking for information about a particular law school, this is the section you want. You'll find here a list of links to schools that are on the Internet (see the first entry below) as well as individual entries for schools with outstanding sites.

A List of Law Schools on the Internet

http://www.usc.edu/dept/law-lib/librarys/locators.html

This site, from the USC (University of Southern California) law library, is a list of links to law schools that have an Internet presence, whether it be a World Wide Web or Gopher site (Figure 2.20). If you want information about a specific school or schools, look here; the list is comprehensive and frequently updated. At the time of this writing, you could access 149 law schools all over the world from this site.

Index of Law School Web and Gopher Servers

This index is a service of the USC Law Library.
Last Updated - May 25, 1995
Return to the USC Law Center Home Page

1. American University Washington College of Law
2. Australian Legal Information Institute (AustLII) - operated jointly by the University of New South Wales (UNSW) and the University of Technology, Sydney (UTS).
3. Boston College Law School Library
4. Boston University School of Law
5. Case Western Reserve University Law School
6. Catholic University of America Columbus School of Law
7. Chicago-Kent College of Law
8. Chicago Kent College of Law Library
9. City University of New York School of Law at Queens College
10. Cleveland State University Law School
11. College of William and Mary Marshall-Wyth School of Law
12. Columbia University School of Law
13. Columbia Law Library's LawNet -Telnet
14. Cornell Law School and the Legal Information Institute (LII).
15. Creighton University School of Law

Figure 2.20:
Part of a list of law schools on the Internet

Queen's University of Belfast Law School

http://www.law.qub.ac.uk/default.htm

This is quite a good Web page from the law school of Queen's University in Belfast, Northern Ireland. I like it because it takes advantage of what the World Wide Web can do. It uses both textual and graphical elements and it provides (or provides links to) a lot of information (Figure 2.21).

There is, of course, information about the law school itself and its faculty. As an American lawyer though, what caught my eye was a chapter from a book called *The Legal System of Northern Ireland*, by a law professor at the University of Ulster named Brice Dickson. The chapter gives a short history

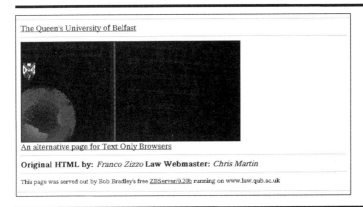

The Queen's University of Belfast

An alternative page for Text Only Browsers

Original HTML by: *Franco Zizzo* **Law Webmaster:** *Chris Martin*

This page was served out by Bob Bradley's free ZBServer/0.20b running on www.law.qub.ac.uk

Figure 2.21:
The Faculty and School of Law, Queen's University, Belfast, Northern Ireland

of the Northern Irish legal system, an explanation of its structure, and how it differs from the English system, all of which I know precious little about.

Another standout is the States of Emergency database, which gives information about "declared and de facto" states of emergency in countries around the world, including relevant legislation and judicial decisions. All of this, and links to legal information world-wide, make the Queen's University page worth a number of visits.

What Is a Tort?

And why, my friend asks, isn't it something I get at a bakery? The standard definition you get in a first-year-in-law-school Torts class is something like "a noncontractual, civil wrong." The definition given in *Black's Law Dictionary* is a little clearer: "A legal wrong committed upon the person or property independent of contract." Both definitions need to be unpacked a bit.

First, a tort is a civil, not a criminal, wrong (see the sidebar *Civil Cases v. Criminal Cases* near the beginning of Part Two). Tort cases can be brought to court directly by the injured party against the "tort-feasor," the one that committed the tort, and the injured party usually seeks money damages. Putting the tort-feasor in jail is not an option.

Second, if someone does not live up to their contractual obligations, you usually can't sue them for a tort. (You can sue them for breach of contract.) This is why torts are said to be noncontractual or independent of contract. In recent years, this historically sharp distinction has blurred a little bit. It is possible, under certain conditions, to sue someone for the tort of breaching a contract in bad faith.

Finally, the torts themselves, the legal wrongs committed upon person or property, come in a few different flavors. There are so-called intentional torts, which involve intentional harm to person or property. These include assault, battery, false imprisonment, and trespass. You can also commit a tort by being negligent, which involves injuring through insufficient care, even though you don't intend any harm. There are many other torts, too many to mention here, but some of them, notably libel, slander, and making defective products ("product liability"), make the news frequently.

Rutgers University-Newark: Ackerson Law Library

http://www.rutgers.edu/lawschool.html

Here is quite a long page from the Ackerson Law Library at the Rutgers University Law School in Newark, New Jersey. The page provides information about the library, includes a Telnet link to its online catalog, and comprises quite a large number of law-related links. You'll find links to information on the World Wide Web and on Gopher, links to law firms and legal and government organizations, links to different legal subjects, and more.

University of Alberta Faculty of Law

http://gpu.srv.ualberta.ca/~law/law.html

Don't be misled by the use of the word "faculty" here—it is used in its European sense, meaning "school" or "college," not a roster of professors. The Law Faculty's Web page is quite a good one. It provides a lot of information about the school itself: a brief tour, profiles of its faculty (including e-mail addresses), admissions information (such as requirements and answers to frequently asked questions), and course listings. (Course descriptions are promised but were not yet available as of this writing.) See Figure 2.22.

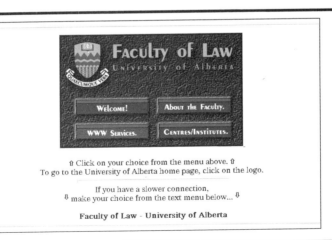

Figure 2.22:
The Faculty (i.e., School or College) of Law at the University of Alberta

This page isn't just an electronic brochure, though. It has a couple of features that really take advantage of the medium, and law professors in particular should take note. If you follow the link to The Electronic Easement, you will find what is intended to be a forum for teachers of property and trust law to exchange (and have posted here) information such as teaching materials and articles. There is also course information for students enrolled in classes. One professor of evidence law—in fact the only professor so far to take advantage of the school's Web page—has posted a course syllabus and outlines of the material covered.

Law professors and teachers interested in using computers and the Internet as teaching tools should also look at the entries under the "Information for Law Teachers" heading below. (Also take a look at the Tax World entry under the "Taxes" heading of "Have a Problem? Check Here First!" earlier in Part Two.)

The USC Law Library and Law Center

http://www.usc.edu/dept/law-lib/usclaw.html

Here is quite a good page from the University of Southern California Law Library and Law Center. You find your basic "who and what we are" information here, such as library hours, staff listings, and a Telnet link to the library catalog, and you'll also find links to all sorts of legal information on the Internet. The links are broken down by category, so whether you're looking for subject information (links to anything from "Administrative Law" to "Women and the Law"), or for California law, international and foreign law, government information, online law journals, or even job listings, you're likely to find something here.

INFORMATION FOR LAW TEACHERS

The sites in this section will be of interest to law professors and law teachers interested in using the computer as a teaching and research tool.

Law Firms on the Internet

Law firms are rapidly finding their way onto the Internet as a means of improving communication between lawyers as well as between firms and their clients. The Internet also offers law firms an easy vehicle for attracting new business. There are a few firms listed on the List of Law Schools on the Internet page discussed earlier in this section, and even more on on a Web page located at

http://www.law.indiana.edu/law/lawfirms.html

which presents an alphabetical list of law firms.

Attorneys or firms that would like to get on the Internet but do not have the time or know-how to do so should check out The Seamless WEBsite™, which will design and maintain a World Wide Web page for you. Their entry is under the "Commercial Services for Lawyers" heading of my "Lawyer's Desk Reference" section.

Many firms treat the Internet as just another means of advertising, so their sites only give you the basic Ps and Qs of the firm itself: where it's located, what areas it practices in, who its attorneys are, and so forth. Some firms, though, see more potential in their sites. One particularly outstanding site I found is from Brickler & Eckler, a Columbus, Ohio law firm. Not only do they provide firm and attorney information, but their Web page provides links to other law-related information on the Internet and copies of publications written by the firm's attorneys, from legal briefs to journal and magazine articles. The URL for Bricker & Eckler is

http://benet-np1.bricker.com/welcome.htm

Another outstanding site is one belonging to The Alexander Law Firm's Consumer Law Page™, which I discuss under the "Consumer Protection" heading of my section "Have a Problem? Check Here First!".

Those interested in using the Internet as a teaching tool should also look at two good uses of the World Wide Web: the Tax World page (under the "Taxes" heading of my section "Have a Problem? Check Here First!") and the University of Alberta Faculty of Law page (under the heading "Law Schools on the Internet" in my section "Checking Out Law Schools and Law Libraries").

Computer Aided Legal Instruction

cali.kentlaw.edu

The Center for Computer Aided Legal Instruction (CALI) at the University of Minnesota provides computer exercises to participating law schools. Take a look at this Gopher site if you want more information. You'll find subscription information, a catalog of programs offered, and subjects covered (approximately twenty subject areas, from Accounting to Wills and Trusts). There's also a demonstration program available for download.

There is a CALI list mailing available. You can subscribe by sending the message

subscribe CALI-L yourfirstname yourlastname

to the following address:

listserver@CALI.kentlaw.edu

However, I monitored the list for about six weeks earlier this year and not a single message was posted.

ProbNET

http://www.law.vill.edu/vls/probnet/

ProbNET is an opportunity for legal-writing teachers to exchange legal writing problems, fact patterns, tests, etc. If you are interested, you should send e-mail to the contact given on this Web page. Materials are available by FTP but require a password, to prevent unauthorized students from obtaining tests.

LAW LIBRARY CATALOGS ON THE INTERNET

Being able to log in to a library catalog from your desk at home is a real convenience. I've listed here the Telnet addresses and login names for the online library catalogs of some of the more renowned law schools in the country (see Table 2.1). More comprehensive lists of Internet-accessible law library catalogs may be found on the Web pages listed below. The sites in this section provide links to law library catalogs throughout the country.

Law Library Catalogs

http://law.wuacc.edu/washlaw/lawcat/lawcat3m.html

This Web page comes from the Washburn University School of Law. It is a good-sized list of links to law library catalogs nationwide. Connections to the catalogs are made via Telnet (Figure 2.23), so you must have a stand-alone

Table 2.1: Telnet Addresses for Some of the More Renowned American Law School Libraries		
Library	**Telnet Address**	**Log In As**
Columbia University Law Library	pegasus.law.columbia.edu	pegasus
Georgetown University Law Library	141.161.38.45	gull
Harvard On-line Library Information System	hollis.harvard.edu	hollis
Stanford University Law Library	forsythetn.stanford.edu	socrates
UCLA Law Library	melvyl.cop.edu	(not needed)
University of Minnesota Libraries	lumina.lib.umn.edu	(not needed)
University of Texas Tarlton Law Library	tallons.law.utexas.edu	tallons
University of California Boalt Law Library	128.32.233.176 or cat.law.berkeley.edu	library
University of Chicago Libraries	libcat.uchicago.edu	(not needed)
University of Colorado Law Library	128.138.161.92 or wpac.colorado.edu	(not needed)
University of Michigan Law Library	lexcalibur.lib.law.umich.edu	(not needed)
University of Pennsylvania Law Library	lola.law.upenn.edu	lola
University of Virginia Law Library	innopac.law.virginia.edu	library
University of Washington (UWIN)	140.142.45.2 or uwin.u.washington.edu	(not needed)
Yale Law School, Lillian Goldman Law Library	130.132.84.29 or ringding.law.yale.edu	morris or library

Telnet program on your computer and your Web browser must be set up to access it.

http://www.pls.com:8001/d2/kelli/httpd/htdocs/his/114.GBM

The House of Representatives Internet Law Library also has a page of links to law libraries. This page contains a few different links than the Washburn page above, including some overseas libraries.

```
                Welcome to the BOALT ON-LINE CATALOG   BOALT LAW LIBRARY

You may search for library materials by any of the following:

        A > AUTHOR
        T > TITLE
        S > SUBJECT
        C > CALL NO
        G > GOVT DOC#

        W > WORDS in title or in corporate name
        R > RESERVE Lists
        I > Library INFORMATION


        D > DISCONNECT
            Choose one (A,T,S,C,G,W,R,I,D)
For further assistance, please see the nice folks at the REFERENCE DESK.
```

Figure 2.23:
The main menu of the Boalt Hall law library catalog at the University of California, Berkeley

More Law Library Catalogs

info.tamu.edu

This list of links to law library catalogs (see also the entry above) is found on a Gopher server at Texas A & M University under the the heading Browse by Subject (confusingly, there are two "Browse by Subject" heads on the main menu—select the bottom one), then Law, and finally Law Libraries.

If you're using a Web browser, you can go directly to the library list without stepping through the Gopher menus. Use the following URL:

gopher://info.tamu.edu:70/11/.dir/lawlib.dir

Since you access law library catalogs through Telnet, your system must have a Telnet program installed and configured in order to be able to access the catalogs from this list.

The Federal Government and U.S. Law

These days, the federal government makes a lot of information available electronically. There are government entries in other sections in this book, such as the IRS, the Social Security Administration, or the Copyright Office, but these sites tend to fall under a specific subject heading. The government sites in this section, by contrast, are generally about the government itself. Some are concerned with the federal government as a whole, and others with one of the three branches: executive, legislative, and judicial.

If you've already checked out the IRS site presented earlier in Part Two (under the heading "Taxes," of course, in my "Have a Problem? Check Here First!" section), you've seen that the government is capable of producing excellent Internet sites; so it should be no surprise that the collection here contains a few gems. In this section be sure especially to check out the U.S. Government Manual site and THOMAS.

ABOUT THE FEDERAL GOVERNMENT

The sites in this section deal with the federal government as a whole. You'll find sites particular to the executive, legislative, and judicial branches in the three subsections following this one.

The Federal Web Locator

http://www.law.vill.edu/Fed-Agency/fedwebloc.html

This very large (just over 80,000 bytes) Web page from the Villanova Center for Information Law and Public Policy is a complete list of links to federal government World Wide Web sites (and it even has a few non-Web sites as well, including the House and Senate Gophers). If you're looking for federal government information on the Web, this is the place to go.

As much as I like the fact that the list here is complete, I do have some minor reservations. First, there are links to sites from most cabinet departments and many agencies, so the information available to you covers, as you can imagine, many different subjects. There are going to be big blocks of links far afield from your interests. Second, the page is not well indexed and it is easy to lose track of where you are. Since the list is so large, then, it is awkward to use; it would be better to break it up into a number of separate pages.

FedWorld

http://www.fedworld.gov

This is a Web page from the National Technical Information Service that aims to provide a "central access" point to government information. It contains a good number of links indexed alphabetically by subject. Under Justice, Law and Treasury, for example, I found links to a number of sites included in this book, such as the U.S. Patent Act, the U.S. Patent and Trademark Office, and decisions of the U.S. Court of Appeals for the Eleventh Circuit.

I don't think there are as many links as there are on the Federal Web Locator (see the entry above), but its subject index makes FedWorld much easier to use if you want government information.

The Internet Wiretap Civics and Government Archive

wiretap.spies.com

This Gopher site has an interesting and eclectic collection of government information under the entry Government Docs (US & World). You'll find things here that don't show up in too many other places, such as different political party platforms or the text of prominent federal laws like the Brady Bill and the Americans with Disabilities Act (Figure 2.24).

Since the collection is so varied, it's a good thing it is searchable. You'll find its search program under the About the Internet Wiretap entry on the main Gopher menu (i.e., the same one where you found Government Docs (US & World)).

```
  ! README (wiretap.spies.com)
  Americans with Disabilities Act
  Australian Law Documents
  Bills before U.S. Congress (limited)
  Brady Handgun Violence Prevention Act
  Canadian Documents
  Citizen's Guide to using the FOIA
  Civil Forfeiture of Assets
  Clinton's Economic Plan
  Copyright
  Electronic Communications Privacy Act
  Fair Credit Reporting Act
  GAO High Risk Reports
  GAO Miscellaneous
  GAO Technical Reports
  GAO Transition Reports
  Gore's National Performance Review Report
  Maastricht Treaty of European Union
  Miscellaneous World Documents
```

Figure 2.24:
Part of Wiretap's varied Civics and Government collection

Check out the international documents here as well. These are just as varied as the U.S. documents—anything from the full text of the NATO Handbook *to the Maastricht Treaty on European Union.*

The U.S. Government Manual

una.hh.lib.umich.edu

The *U.S. Government Manual* is the official handbook of the federal government. I've known it for some time as the thick paperback book that I often borrow from the reserve desk at the law library. I was very happy to discover that the full text of the manual is available on line at this Gopher site at the University of Michigan, under the entries socsci, Government, and U.S. Government Manual 1994/95.

If you are using a Web browser, you can go directly to the Manual without stepping through the Gopher entries. Use the URL:

gopher://una.hh.lib.umich.edu:70/11/socsci/poliscilaw/govman

The Manual is a comprehensive reference of the federal government. It describes what every government branch, department, court, agency, and sub-agency does, giving also a brief history, a list of officials, and addresses and phone numbers (Figure 2.25). There is even an appendix describing government agencies that no longer exist. As implemented here, the Manual is searchable, a nice feature since there is quite a lot of information to manage.

My only regrets are that the illustrations found in the printed Manual are not available and that tables are not well aligned (and some even appear scrambled).

THE EXECUTIVE BRANCH

The sites in this section contain information about and information produced by the executive branch of the federal government (the president, the cabinet department, and executive agencies).

The Department of Justice

justice2.usdoj.gov

The Department of Justice Gopher contains a nice mix of information. You'll find some information about the department, press releases, job listings

---

The Sergeant at Arms maintains the order of the House under the direction of the Speaker and is the keeper of the Mace. As a member of the U.S. Capitol Police Board, the Sergeant at Arms is the chief law enforcement officer for the House and ser ves as Board Chairman each even year. The ceremonial and protocol duties parallel those of the Senate Sergeant at Arms and include arranging the inauguration of the President of the United States, Joint Sessions of Congress, visits to the House of heads o f state, and funerals of Members of Congress.

The Doorkeeper enforces the rules relating to the privileges of the Hall of the House, including admission to the galleries. The Doorkeeper is also responsible for the distribution of House documents and supervises the operations of the House Do cument Room.

The Director of Nonlegislative and Financial Services is charged with the administration of other House support services including payroll, benefits, postal operations and internal mail distribution, office furnishings, office equipment, and off ice supplies. The Director is appointed jointly by the Speaker, the Majority Leader, and the Minority Leader.

Figure 2.25:
Descriptions of some of the elected officers of the House of Representatives, from the U.S. Government Manual

Famous Supreme Court Cases: Griswold v. Connecticut

As late as 1968 Connecticut had a statute on its books prohibiting the use of "any drug, medicinal article or instrument for the purpose of preventing conception."

The law was challenged by Griswold, the executive director of the Planned Parenthood League of Connecticut on behalf of married patients using contraceptives. They were both found guilty—as accessories—of violating the Connecticut anti-contraception law; they had given "information, instruction, and medical advice to married persons as to the means of preventing conception."

The Supreme Court struck down the Connecticut law, not because it violated any particular provision of the Constitution, but rather because it offended a right of freedom from government intrusion into private matters—in short, a right of privacy—implicit in many provisions of the Bill of Rights. Justice William O. Douglas wrote for the Court: "Would we allow the police to search the sacred precincts of marital bedrooms for telltale signs of the use of contraceptives? The very idea is repulsive to the notions of privacy surrounding the marriage relationship."

(both for attorneys and non-attorneys) and so on. However, if you are looking for a basic primer on the DOJ, what it is and what it does, you may not find as much information as you might like.

The material available here from the different divisions of the DOJ, though, is really worth a look. The major divisions, such as Antitrust, Civil Rights, and the FBI, publish information about prominent cases they handle. You'll find, for example, copies of the court documents filed in the Microsoft antitrust case (Figure 2.26) and in the Denny's Restaurant discrimination case. You'll also find information from the FBI about both the Unabomber and Oklahoma City bombing cases, including sketches of suspects. If you're interested in newsmaking government cases (and even some that aren't), you'll find this a valuable site.

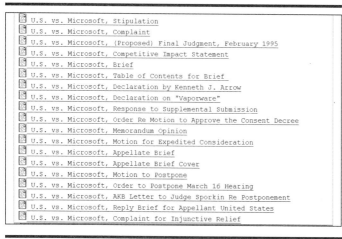

Figure 2.26:
Documents filed by the Justice Department in the Microsoft antitrust case

The Federal Register

gopher.nara.gov

The *Federal Register* is the daily bulletin of the executive branch. All rules and regulations, proposed rules and regulations, orders, and notices issued by the president, the cabinet departments, and executive agencies are published there. The Register is available, unfortunately only in part, on this Gopher site from the National Archives, under the entry The Federal Register.

This Gopher site also doubles as a Web page. You can access it at the URL

http://gopher.nara.gov:70/1/register

The full text of the Federal Register is not available on line. What you will find here is the Register's daily table of contents, from January 1, 1994 through yesterday (if yesterday was a business day). The tables of contents for 1995 are grouped together by month and each month of tables is WAIS searchable. For 1994, you can WAIS search through the tables for the entire year. This is a lot faster than using the Register's printed indexes, particularly for material published recently, i.e., since the most recent index (the indexes are printed quarterly).

So, if you use the Federal Register, this site isn't going to save you a trip to the library. The searchable tables of contents, however, can shorten the time you need to spend there.

Securities and Exchange Commision EDGAR Filings

http://town.hall.org/edgar/edgar.html

Corporations that issue securities are required to make regular disclosures of information to the Securities and Exchange Commission (SEC), including such things as quarterly and annual financial statements, or acquisitions of other corporations. Indeed, corporations must report "any material events or corporate changes" that are important to investors or securities holders. These disclosures may be filed with the SEC the old-fashioned way—on paper—or electronically by EDGAR, the SEC's electronic filing system.

This site makes available the full text of all EDGAR filings from the beginning of 1994. Figure 2.27 shows part of the title page of a Microsoft filing.

Finding information is made easy for you here. You can use the built-in search program to look for key words. To guide your search, there are indexes of corporate filings (an index of daily filings and a complete master index), which tell you which corporations filed what forms when. Since the

```
                        UNITED STATES
              SECURITIES AND EXCHANGE COMMISSION
                     WASHINGTON, D.C.  20549

                      -------------

                        FORM 10-Q

[X]   QUARTERLY REPORT PURSUANT TO SECTION 13 OR 15(d)
          OF THE SECURITIES EXCHANGE ACT OF 1934

      FOR THE QUARTERLY PERIOD ENDED DECEMBER 31, 1994


[ ]   TRANSITION REPORT PURSUANT TO SECTION 13 OR 15(d)
          OF THE SECURITIES EXCHANGE ACT OF 1934


      FOR THE TRANSITION PERIOD FROM _____ TO ____

                      -------------

        Commission File Number 0-14278

          MICROSOFT CORPORATION
```

Figure 2.27:
Part of the title page of a Microsoft form 10-Q, a quarterly report filed with the SEC on December 31, 1994

forms have such descriptive names as "3," "8-K," and "10-Q," there is a guide that contains the SEC's explanation of each form.

If you're an investor or potential investor who wants more financial information about a corporation than is disclosed in its annual report to shareholders, take a look here for the corporation's recent SEC filings. In fact, anyone who wants to see recent SEC filings should check out this site.

U.S. Government Resources: Executive Branch

http://www.acm.uiuc.edu/rml/executive-govt.html

This page at the University of Illinois Urbana-Champaign Association for Computing Machinery offers a large list of links to executive branch Internet sites. You'll find links to the White House, to eight of the cabinet departments (and maybe more by the time you read this), and to a fair number of executive agencies, including NASA, EPA, and NSF.

There are also links—and these I found more immediately interesting—to White House documents and information like the 1996 proposed budget, inaugural and State of the Union addresses, presidential radio addresses, and executive orders.

This page is actually linked to (and part of) a larger collection of government resources, which has pages of legislative and judicial branch links as well. I group this site under the executive branch rather than under the "About the Federal Government" heading, above, because I thought the executive branch page here stronger than the legislative and judicial pages.

THE LEGISLATIVE BRANCH

If you want to contact your representatives and senators, or if you want to know exactly what the Congress is doing and when, then take a look at the sites in this section.

Famous Supreme Court Cases: Marbury v. Madison

William Marbury was appointed as a justice of the peace by John Adams in the very last days of his presidency, and Marbury was confirmed by the Senate (as appointments to senior federal offices must be, under the Constitution). For political reasons, however, incoming president Thomas Jefferson and his secretary of state, James Madison, refused to deliver Marbury's commission, which was necessary for him to take office. So Marbury and other late Adams appointees in the same situation went to court, seeking the delivery of their commissions. The result was *Marbury v. Madison*, arguably the most significant case in the history of American constitutional law.

The funny thing about *Marbury*, though, is that the main holding in the case—the legal principle for which the case stands—has nothing to do with the facts in the case. Instead, *Marbury v. Madison* established the power of judicial review in the federal courts. This is the power that the courts have to determine whether or not laws are constitutional and to strike down or nullify those that are not. As then chief justice John Marshall wrote in the *Marbury* opinion: "Thus, the particular phraseology of the constitution of the United States confirms and strengthens the principle ... that a law repugnant to the constitution is void, and that courts, as well as other departments, are bound by that instrument." When you hear on the news, then, that the Supreme Court struck down a law, it is exercising a power formally established in this case back in 1803.

Oh, yes. As for Mr. Marbury, he was out of luck. The Court also ruled that it did not have the power to order the delivery of his commission.

A Congressional Directory

una.hh.lib.umich.edu

There are any number of Congressional directories available on the Internet, including those on the House Web page, House Gopher, and Senate Gopher, below. I like this one from the University of Michigan the best because it puts mailing addresses, phone numbers, fax numbers, and e-mail addresses all in one place. There is a complete listing for the House and Senate, and a listing for the Congressional delegation from each state under the headings soc-sci, Government, U.S. Government: Legislative Branch, and finally Directories of 104th Congress, 1995/96 (see Figure 2.28).

If you are using a Web browser, you can go directly to the directory listings. Use the URL:

gopher://una.hh.lib.umich.edu:70/11/socsci/poliscilaw/uslegi/congdir

The Congressional directory listings are also available for download by FTP. Use the following address:

una.hh.lib.umich.edu

The complete House and Senate directories are in files named hou95 and sen95 in the following directory:

/socsci/poliscilaw/uslegi/congdir

```
                        NEW JERSEY


    Senate Abbreviations            House Abbreviations

    DSOB=Dirksen Senate Office Bldg.  Cannon=Cannon Bldg.
    HSOB=Hart Senate Office Bldg.     LHOB=Longworth House Office Bldg.
    RSOB=Russell Senate Office Bldg.  RHOB=Rayburn House Office Bldg.
    Washington, D.C. 20510            Address: Washington, D.C. 20515

    E-Mail correspondence may be limited to constituents.  Include your
    mailing address with your e-mail message if a reply is desired.


                        SENATORS

    P ST Name and Address         Phone & E-Mail  Fax
    = == =======================  ==============  ==============

    D NJ Bradley, William         1-202-224-3224  1-202-224-8567
         731 HSOB

    D NJ Lautenberg, Frank R.     1-202-224-4744  1-202-224-9707
         506 HSOB
```

Figure 2.28:
Part of the listing for New Jersey's Congressional delegation

The listings by state are in the following directory, where each state has its own file:

/socsci/poliscilaw/uslegi/congdir/state

The House of Representatives Gopher

gopher.house.gov

The House Gopher has some information you'll also find on the House Web page in the entry below, such as the weekly floor schedule and House members' e-mail addresses. There is enough unique information here, though, to list the House Gopher separately.

You'll find, among some other things, information about the leadership of both parties in the House and copies of their speeches and press releases. What I particularly like and what I think particularly useful, though, is the information available for individual representatives. Once you wade past the biographies and the copies of speeches, you find information about special services different representatives offer their constituents (at least those representatives who chose to list themselves on the Gopher; not all the members of the House have done so). Your representative can help you with things like getting a passport quickly, resolving difficulties you might be having with Social Security, and nominating high-school students for one of the military academies. If you want to know what your representative can do for you, look here.

The House of Representatives Web Page

http://www.house.gov

If you want to know about the House of Representatives and what it's doing these days, take a look at the House Web page. You'll find a lot of information here; indeed, you might find more than you expect or want.

You'll find things such as the House calendar, a weekly schedule of what's up for consideration on the House floor, and House members' addresses (e-mail and postal mail). More substantively, you'll find a summary of what's happened on the House floor in the last three days, a description of the jurisdiction of every House committee, and the full text of everything proposed or passed in the House so far this session. In short, if you want to know in detail about what goes on in the House, connect here.

The Senate Gopher

ftp.senate.gov

I've included the Senate Gopher for the sake of completeness, but it really doesn't stack up very well next to either the House Gopher or House Web page. You'll find a list of senators and their mailing address (both postal mail and e-mail), and you can find Senate committee membership lists. Other than this though, you won't find much more than speeches and miscellaneous statements made by members on the Senate floor and in committee.

One nice feature here is that you can search all of the documents. I just wish there were more to search for.

THOMAS

http://thomas.loc.gov/

You'll find some outstanding things at this rich and excellent site, named for Thomas Jefferson. In particular, you'll find the full text of legislation and of the Congressional Record, beginning with the 103rd Congress. You'll also find links to major bills currently under consideration or recently passed, an essay on how laws are made, and links to other legislative sites on the Internet (Figure 2.29).

The legislation material on THOMAS is excellent. It is fully searchable and contains all bills from both the House and Senate. That is, you can find all bills passed by both houses and sent to the president for signature (so-called "enrolled" bills) and also bills introduced in or acted upon only in one chamber or the other. The Congressional Record (the full text of proceedings on both the House and Senate floors) is similarly appealing. You

In the spirit of Thomas Jefferson,
a service of the U.S. Congress through its Library.

- **Full Text of Legislation**
  Full text of all versions of House and Senate bills searchable by keyword(s) or by bill number.
  - ☐ 103rd Congress Bills
  - ☐ 104th Congress Bills

- **Full Text of the Congressional Record**
  - ☐ Congressional Record for the 103rd Congress
  - ☐ Congressional Record for the 104th Congress
  - ☐ Congressional Record Index for the 104th Congress

  Full text of the daily account of proceedings on the House and Senate Floors searchable by keyword(s).

Figure 2.27:
THOMAS (Jefferson)
and links to bills and to
the Congressional
Record, beginning with
the 103rd Congress

can do a full-text search of the proceedings in both chambers, in one chamber, or by speaker or date.

If you're interested in what goes on in Congress and you want up-to-the minute material, not to mention legislative information on the Internet generally, take a look at THOMAS.

THE JUDICIAL BRANCH

The site in this section contains information about the judicial branch. If you want to know about the federal courts, this is the place to look.

The Federal Judiciary

http://www.uscourts.gov

This site is brought to you by the Administrative Office of the United States Courts, which manages such things as the courts' budget matters and legislative agenda. The stated purpose of the site is to provide a "clearinghouse for information from and about the judicial branch of the United States Government." The site is pretty good, although the information "about" the courts is stronger than the information "from" the courts.

If you want to know about the federal courts and how they work, then you should read the online publication called *Understanding the Federal Courts*, available at this site. This will not only tell you about the structure and composition of the Supreme, Circuit, and District courts, but also about less commonly known courts and offices, such as the Magistrate Judges and the Court of Federal Claims.

As I mentioned above, the information here *from* the courts is not as helpful, in part because there isn't much of it. You'll find a few articles from *The Third Branch*, a monthly newsletter from the courts, and a handful of press releases dating from January, 1995 forward.

A Thumbnail Sketch of Supreme Court Opinions

The Supreme Court decides its cases by a simple majority vote of its nine justices. The chief justice assigns one justice to write the opinion of the Court or, if the chief justice does not vote with the majority, the opinion is assigned by the member of the majority who has served on the Court the longest.

Any other justice may write an opinion as well, whether or not he or she voted with the majority. If a justice votes with the majority and writes a separate opinion, what you get is a "concurring opinion." A justice usually writes a concurring opinion when he or she agrees with the result in a case but not with all of the majority's reasoning, or because he or she agrees with the majority's reasoning but feels there is more that should be said. "Dissenting opinions" are written by justices who do not vote with the majority and do not agree with their reasoning.

It is possible in theory to have a case with nine separate opinions written by nine separate justices, and indeed this happened once in the famous Pentagon Papers case, decided in four days under extremely unusual circumstances at the end of June 1971. Usually, however, a case will have four or fewer opinions.

Getting a Case before the U.S. Supreme Court

News coverage of the U.S. Supreme Court usually focuses on the legal and political effects of its important decisions, and rightly so, but readers are often left to wonder how a case gets to the Supreme Court in the first place. It can happen in one of three ways: a case may begin there, it may come by appeal, or it may come by *writ of certiorari*.

The Constitution (Article III, Section 2) and federal law give the Supreme Court *original jurisdiction* over a few kinds of cases. Suits between two state governments begin at the Supreme Court and not in the federal trial court (or "district court") as other cases do. The recent dispute between New York and New Jersey over the location of the Statue of Liberty is one such case, but there aren't many.

Federal law also creates a very few kinds of cases that are tried before a special panel of three district court judges instead of the usual one judge. Appeals in these cases go directly to the Supreme Court and not to the federal courts of appeal (the "Circuit" courts), as is usually the case. Only a very few cases reach the Supreme Court by this avenue.

Nearly all cases reach the Court by *writ of certiorari* (sometimes just called *cert*). With the exception of the few cases described above, the Court has complete discretion over which cases it will hear, and the writ of certiorari is the legal device the Court uses to select them.

Only after your case is heard by a federal Circuit Court or by the supreme court of a state can you "petition" the U.S. Supreme Court for a *writ of cert*. The justices review and vote on all petitions. It takes a vote of four or more justices to grant your petition and hear your case. The Court receives over 7,000 petitions each year and grants fewer than 100.

State Law on the Internet

Just as with the federal government, there is a great deal of state government information available on the Internet, and seemingly more is available every day. As you might expect, what's out there is a mixed bag. Some states seem barely aware of the Internet. For these states, you might find a site or two somewhere with the text of a few laws about telecommunications. Other states make much better use of available technology and provide government information and the full text of court decisions and statutes on the Internet. These latter, better sites are the ones collected in this section.

The Alaska Legal Resource Center

http://touchngo.com/lglcntr/lglcntr.html

The Last Frontier has staked itself a new claim—on the electronic frontier. The Alaska Law Center presents the full text of decisions from the Alaska Supreme Court (February 1995 to the present) and from the Alaska Court of Appeals (also February 1995 to the present). Figure 2.30 shows the title page of a recent Alaska Supreme Court decision. There is also space for Alaska attorneys and other legal service providers to advertise their services. As of this writing, however, only a few have done so.

Attorneys: The court decisions on the Alaska Law Center are official. The text of the decisions are provided by the Alaska courts themselves, subject to corrections made before publication in the Pacific Reporter.

The Center has one pervasive annoyance. One of its sponsors is a corporation called Touch N' Go Systems, which hawks its Windows billing program and other services at every available opportunity—on every Web page. You have to be willing to wade through these ads to get what you want, but it's usually worth it.

```
Notice:    This  is  subject  to  formal  correction   before
publication in the Pacific Reporter.  Readers are  requested
to  bring  errors  to  the attention  of  the  Clerk  of  the
Appellate  Courts,  303 K Street, Anchorage,  Alaska  99501,
(907) 264-0607.


        THE SUPREME COURT OF THE STATE OF ALASKA

A.H.,                         )
                              )      Supreme Court File No. S-5683
             Appellant,       )
                              )      Superior Court File No.
                              )      3AN-87-11173 Civil
         v.                   )
                              )
W.P.,                         )      O P I N I O N
                              )
             Appellee.    )      [No. 4222 - June  9,  1995]
)


         Appeal from the Superior Court  of  the
    State  of  Alaska,  Third Judicial  District,
    Anchorage,
```

Figure 2.30:
The title page from a
recent Alaska Supreme
Court child custody
decision

California Codes

http://www.law.indiana.edu/codes/ca/codes.html

This Web site gives you access to the full text of California laws, which makes it a useful reference. You'll find a link to each separate code—California organizes its laws into codes by subject: Business & Professions Code, Civil Code, Penal Code, etc.—and for each code there is a detailed and descriptive table of contents. Links to the text of each individual section state the first line of the section itself.

If you want to download the California codes (as opposed to merely reading them on screen) you can find them available for FTP at a California state government site. The address is leginfo.public.ca.gov *and the codes are in the* /pub/code *directory.*

Unfortunately, the codes are not searchable, so if you are not familiar with the codes it may be difficult for you to find a particular provision.

Practitioners should note that the codes are not official and do not contain annotations. They are useful for reference but not as a research tool.

California Legislative Information

scilibx.ucsc.edu

AB 1624, signed into law in October 1993, directed the California Legislature to make available electronically "specified information concerning bills, the proceedings of the houses and committees of the Legislature, statutory enactments, and the California Constitution." You'll find this legislative information on a Gopher site at the University of California, Santa Cruz, under the entries The Government and California Leglislative Information.

There is a lot of information here, of which the most interesting, perhaps, is the bills. Beginning with the 1993/94 session, you'll find the full text of every bill introduced into either chamber of the California Legislature (the Assembly or the Senate), the history of each bill in committee and on the floor, and the results of committee and floor votes. Bills are indexed by bill number and by author and are fully searchable. You'll also find such things as the legislative calendar and the full text of the state constitution (which is quite long). If you like to keep track of current California legislation, this is the place to look.

Users of Web browsers won't save much time by going directly to the legislative information instead of stepping through Gopher menu entries. However, if you'd rather use the Web address, here it is:

gopher://scilibx.ucsc.edu/11/The%20Community/Guide%20to%20GovernmentU.S
.%2c%20State%20and%20Local/California%20Legislative%20Information

The Colorado Legal Alliance

http://usa.net/cololaw/index.htm

This site from the Colorado Legal Alliance aims to put Colorado and national legal resources on line, and it succeeds quite well. If it's Colorado government information you want, you'll find information about the legislature (such as its schedule and state representatives' names and addresses) and information from the governor's office. If you want information on Colorado law, you'll find the current Colorado Revised Statutes (Colorado laws), which are searchable. You'll also find such things as corporation and limited partnership forms, and links to the Colorado Bar Association and to Colorado lawyers who are on line.

First, attorneys should note that the Colorado Revised Statutes available here are not official and do not contain annotations. Second, everyone interested in this site should note that you must register to get access to the statutes. Registration is free and is done on line. You only need to provide your e-mail address (name and postal mail address optional), but you may get unsolicited e-mail, faxes, or mail as a result.

For legal information outside Colorado, there are links to federal sites like the complete United States Code and Congress's THOMAS, as well as other legal information sites on the Internet.

Florida Legislative Information Network

 http://garnet.acns.fsu.edu/~w870g003/

This is an outstanding site; states that are considering the Internet as a means for making their legislative information available to the public should take a look here. If you're interested in Florida law and in keeping tabs on the Florida state legislature, you should check in here as well.

Florida statutes and the Florida constitution are here and are searchable. Bills from the current legislative session are also here and are also searchable. Better still, you can download them. If you want to write to state representatives and senators, you'll find their phone numbers and addresses (both e-mail and postal mail) as well as an essay on writing them effective letters (very handy). Links to this and other information is shown in Figure 2.31.

 Lawyers should note that the Florida statutes and bills are not official and are not annotated.

But wait, there's more! You'll find information on hot topics in the legislature this session, laws recently passed (and when they're slated to go into effect), and even a roster of registered lobbyists. You get the idea. This site is an excellent exercise in public access to government.

Figure 2.31:
The Florida Legislative
Information Network
Home Page

The Indiana Code

http://www.law.indiana.edu/codes/in/incode.html

This site, from the Indiana University School of Law, has the complete Indiana Code and is a handy reference. The code is organized by title (i.e., volume), and each title has a detailed table of contents. The code is also WAIS-searchable, which is good for finding things if you are unfamiliar with the Indiana Code. You can search for any word or words you like, and the built-in search program will respond with a list of links to the statutes that contain what you searched for. For more information on how to compose WAIS searches, see the sidebar *WAIS Searches* in my section "Best Ways of Finding More and Better Sites" at the end of Part Two.

Attorneys should note that the Indiana Code is not official and is not annotated.

Indiana State Bills

http://www.law.indiana.edu/bills/in/inbills.html

This site complements The Indiana Code in the preceding entry. Whereas there you will find the current laws of Indiana, here you will find information on the current legislative session.

The full text of current bills in both the Indiana House and Senate is available here and is fully searchable, which is good, because the bills are only indexed by bill number. (Without the search capability, if you didn't know the bill number, you couldn't find anything).

Bills are available in HTML format. If you have WordPerfect version 5.1 or later, you may be interested to know that the bills are available in WordPerfect 5.1 format as well. The WordPerfect-format bills cannot be downloaded directly, however. Instead, you must first configure your Web browser to start WordPerfect when you select a .WP file. Then, once you've selected the file you want and the bill is displayed in WordPerfect, you can save it.

The Minnesota Legislature

gopher.revisor.leg.state.mn.us

There is a good deal of information about the Minnesota Legislature here. You'll find general descriptions of Minnesota legislative districts; information about television coverage of the legislature, the structure and functions of the legislature, and how a bill becomes law in Minnesota; and the phone numbers and addresses (e-mail and postal mail) of legislators.

You'll also find a good deal of information on bills: the full text and status of all bills introduced in the current legislative session; their current status; and summary lists of bills sent to the governor, those signed into law, and those vetoed. The bill information is not searchable, however, which is a drawback.

If you want to get information on (or a copy of) a bill currently before a state legislature that has not put this information on line, you'll find a list here of the names and phone numbers of the proper office to contact in every state. The list entry is Getting bills from other states; *you'll find it under the* Legislation and bill tracking *entry.*

The New York Court of Appeals

http://www.law.cornell.edu/ny/ctap/overview.html

The New York Court of Appeals has been one of the most prestigious state courts in the country for a good part of this century. The full text of its recent opinions (1992 to the present) may be found in hypertext format at this excellent site from the Legal Information Institute at the Cornell University Law School.

The names New York gives to its courts are a bit unusual. Most states refer to their highest court as the Supreme Court and use "Court of Appeals" to refer to the appellate court below the Supreme Court. In New York, the Court of Appeals is the highest court, the Supreme Court is the trial court, and the Appellate Division of the Supreme Court is the appellate court below the Court of Appeals.

You can find cases you want by doing a WAIS search for key terms (for more information on how to compose WAIS searches, see the sidebar *WAIS Searches* in my section "Best Ways of Finding More and Better Sites" at the end of Part Two) or through the comprehensive topic index, in which you will find everything the court has dealt with, from *abortion* through *zoning*. Also, cases in the current term are listed by date, and cases from prior terms are listed by the names of the parties.

Attorneys should note that the decisions here are not official and are not annotated.

What makes this site truly noteworthy is that the opinions are hypertext documents. Other New York Court of Appeals cases cited as authority in the opinions here appear as links (for an example, see Figure 2.32). These links take you directly to the opinions in the cited cases (assuming those cases are recent and available at this site).

III.

The Appellate Division concluded that the evidence against defendant was legally insufficient to establish that he acted with larcenous intent under the strict standard set forth in Penal Law § 155.05(2)(d). The court's application of that standard and the dissenter's comments on the subject here suggest the need for further discussion about the proper standard for appellate review.

Although the trier of fact in the Norman case was bound to consider the evidence in light of the statutory "moral certainty" standard, the function of an appellate court reviewing the record for legal evidentiary sufficiency under Penal Law § 155.05(2)(d) is limited to assessing whether the inference of wrongful intent logically flowed from the proven facts and whether any valid line of reasoning could lead a rational trier of fact, viewing the evidence in the light most favorable to the People, to conclude that the defendant committed the charged crime (_People v Williams_, 84 NY2d 924; see, _People v Wong_, 81 NY2d 600, 608; _People v Jennings_, 69 NY2d 103; _People v Deegan_, 69 NY2d 976; see also, _People v Geraci_, supra, slip op., at 17- 18). At this level of inquiry, Penal Law § 155.05(2)(d)'s "moral certainty" standard is not an appropriate criterion for measuring the sufficiency of the People's proof.

Contrary to the dissenter's contention, the standard of review we are applying here is not a sudden departure from precedent, but rather is a reflection of well-established principles that have regularly been reiterated in our recent case law. In _People v Deegan_ (69 NY2d 976, 978-979) and _People v Jennings_ (69 NY2d 103, 114-155), we stated that the "moral certainty" standard is only for the trier of fact and that the proper measure of legal sufficiency is whether the facts and the inferences that flow therefrom support a finding for the People on every element of the charged crime. We also stated in _Deegan_ that the availability of innocent inferences is not relevant to the sufficiency inquiry. In so holding, we expressly overruled an older case, _People v Eckert_ (2 NY2d 126, 129), in which the Court stated that the legal sufficiency of circumstantial evidence is determined, as least in part, by whether the facts and inferences "exclude to a moral certainty every other reasonable hypothesis but guilt." We subsequently made clear

Figure 2.32: Part of a recent decision of the New York Court of Appeals. Some of the citations for cases cited as authority are links to other hypertext decisions of the court.

New York Laws and Legislative Information

lbdc.senate.state.ny.us

If you want information on bills under consideration in the current session of the New York state legislature, this is the place to look. Available to you here is the full text of every bill introduced in the current session, along with a short summary of the bill and a statement of its status. This information is all fully searchable by key terms. Indeed, the only way for you to access it is by searching (there are no indexes by bill number or author), but I do not think this is much of a problem.

The complete New York statutes are also available at this site, and if you are already somewhat familiar with them, you might use them here as a reference. Be warned, though: The collected statutes are huge, and although they are organized by title (i.e., subject) and each title has a table of contents, they are not indexed and are not searchable. If you are not familiar with New York statutes it is going to be very hard to find whatever it is you're looking for. I recommend going to a law library if possible.

Utah Information

http://www.gv.ex.state.ut.us/

This Web page presents a nice overall package, although parts of it are still under construction as of this writing. It has a good mix of text and graphics and also of law-related, government, and general information about the state of Utah (see Figure 2.33). It accomplishes its stated purpose, of providing access to the "information resources of Utah government entities," and then some.

The information about the state government on this page is still under construction, so you'll only find short blurbs about, for example, the houses of the state legislature and how laws are made. There are, however, links to a Gopher site containing the full, searchable Utah code, the Utah constitution, and bills introduced in the current legislative session.

The general information about Utah is also nicely done, if you're interested in visiting. You'll find details about Utah's winning bid for the 2002 Winter Olympics, a Utah travel guide, information on conditions at Utah ski resorts (Ski Utah!), and even information for people relocating to the state, including things such as real estate price ranges.

State Government and State Law Sites

http://www.law.indiana.edu/law/states.html

This Web page is part of the World Wide Web Virtual Library at the Indiana University School of Law. It is a large, perhaps comprehensive, list of links to state government and state law information on the Internet. All fifty states are represented and the links will take you not only to Web sites, but to Gopher and Telnet sites as well.

Some states have made a lot of good law-related information available. You will find links to court decisions, legislatures, governor's offices, codes, and constitutions. Some of these states are represented in the other entries in this section. Other states provide more general information, about such things as tourism and natural resources or about government agencies. Still others are under construction.

In short, if you are looking for information from a particular state, you would do well to start looking here. What you're eventually going to find, however is something of a toss-up.

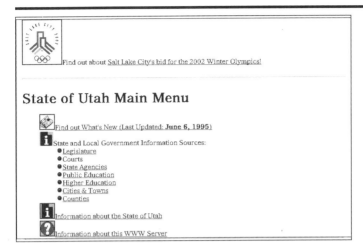

Figure 2.33:
The main menu from the State of Utah home page showing links to government information and Salt Lake City's recent Olympic bid

Famous Supreme Court Cases: Martin v. Hunter's Lessee

This case started out as a dispute about a piece of land in Virginia, one among many seized from British subjects by that state. Hunter claimed the land was granted to him by Virginia in 1789. Martin, a British subject, claimed the grant to Hunter was invalid under treaties between the United States and England that prohibited land confiscation. The case made its way up through the Virginia courts, with the Virginia Court of Appeals finally ruling against Martin. The U.S. Supreme Court reversed and sent the case back to the Virginia court with instructions to enter judgment for Martin.

Had the Virginia court simply done as instructed, that would have been the end of it and this case would likely have faded into early U.S. history. Instead, the Virginia court refused to follow the Supreme Court's instructions, with the result that *Martin v. Hunter's Lessee* (1816) became another fundamental and enduring case in American constitutional law.

The Virginia court held that the U.S. Supreme Court did not have jurisdiction over cases arising in the state courts. The Supreme Court disagreed and reversed the Virginia court again: "On the whole, the court are of the opinion, that the appellate power of the United States does extend to cases pending in the state courts; and that the [statute that] authorizes the exercise of this jurisdiction in the specified cases ... is supported by the letter and spirit of the constitution."

Martin, then, formally established a principle of the American legal system we take for granted today. The U.S. Supreme Court can hear state court cases, as long as they deal with some question of federal or U.S. constitutional law.

Laws of Other Nations

Many of the sites in this book contain information about American law and American government. The Internet is a global network, though, and so it should come as no surprise that legal information from other countries should be available as well.

I have selected a small sample of sites that I think stand out for one reason or another. Canada is well represented on the Internet. You can also find South African and Eastern European constitutional information. In addition, there are "library" sites with links to law-related information from more than 70 countries.

If you are looking for sites on international law—those laws that govern the legal relations between nations, such as international treaties or conventions—see the "International Law" section following this one.

A Constitutional Repository for South Africa

http://pc72.law.wits.ac.za/

This site, maintained by the Law School of the University of the Witwatersrand in Johannesburg, contains information and links to information related to the new South African constitution and the new Constitutional Court (Figure 2.34). There isn't a great deal of information here yet, because the constitution and the Constitutional Court are so new, but what is here is very exciting. You get to watch part of the development of a new constitution and a new rule of law.

You'll find a copy of the new constitution and some of the more important opinions of the Constitutional Court here. Its first-ever decision deals with confessions. Its most recent decision (as of this writing) was front-page news around the world—the death penalty was found to be unconstitutional

Welcome to WITS Law School

Welcome to the Law School Constitutional Repository, University of the Witwatersrand, Johannesburg, South Africa.

Please read our disclaimer.

What we have available at our site:

- South African Constitutional Court Opinions
- Constitutional Documents
- About the Court and the Judges
- Links to other sites of legal interest

Other sites:

- WWW at SUNSITE, WITS
- WWW Servers available in South Africa
- Other WWW Servers in the World

Figure 2.34: The Law School Constitutional Repository, University of the Witwatersrand, Johannesburg, South Africa—with links to South African constitutional documents, court opinions, and information

under the new constitution. The court's decisions are available for download in ASCII, WordPerfect, and Word 6 for Windows format.

You'll also find links to a Gopher site containing the minutes and reports of the Constitutional Assembly that drew up the new constitution, and to other law-related sites on the Internet. If you're interested in South African law and politics, you must take a look at this site.

Canada Open Government Project

http://info.ic.gc.ca/opengov

The purpose of this pilot project from the government of Canada is to provide "greater access to government through information networks." Though still under construction in places, the site makes good use of the World Wide Web, and it accomplishes its purpose pretty well.

The information here, of course, is all about the federal government of Canada, and it's available in English and French (Figure 2.35). You'll find a description of the House of Commons, which political parties are represented there, what the Members of Parliament (MPs) do, and a little help in finding which MP represents which part of the country. You'll also find government documents such as the 1995 federal budget and the Charter of Rights and Freedoms. A particularly nice feature—and something I didn't see at American government sites—was a list of links to Web pages for major

The Senate of Canada
The Senate section provides information about the role of Senators in the Canadian Parliament and contact information for the Senators.

House of Commons
The House of Commons section provides contact information about Members of Parliament and some information about the House itself.

Independently maintained Political Party Home-pages

Supreme Court of Canada
The Supreme Court section provides access to recent rulings of the court, information about the Justices of the Supreme Court, and historical information about the court.

Important Government documents and treaties

☐ Governmental Budgets (Federal and Provincial)

Figure 2.35:
Some of the available links on the Canada Open Government Project page

and minor political parties. There is even a sound file of the Canadian national anthem.

The information is well organized, so the fact that it is searchable is an added bonus. You can search all of the information on this site or search any part of it that you select from a list. (Some information that you can access from this site is located elsewhere, however, and is not searchable.)

The Center for the Study of Constitutionalism in Eastern Europe

lawnext.uchicago.edu

The Center for the Study of Constitutionalism in Eastern Europe was established in 1990, by the University of Chicago Law School and a group of Eastern and Central European universities, to "undertake a multi-year study of the constitution-making process in the post-Communist nations of Eastern and Central Europe...." The Center's Gopher site is part of this Chicago Law School Gopher; it is under the entry Center for the Study of Constitutionalism in Eastern Europe.

You may connect directly to the center if you are using a Web browser. The URL is:

gopher://lawnext.uchicago.edu:70/11/.center

You'll find here the full text of the center's law journal, *The Eastern European Constitutional Review*. It contains, among other things, articles on the problems faced by the former Soviet-bloc countries in drafting and implementing new constitutions and updates on the progress of individual countries' drafting. There is also an archive with draft and final constitutions and bibliographies of relevant articles and books.

If you are at all interested in Eastern European constitutional scholarship, you should check in here.

Government of Canada

gopher.nlc-bnc.ca

This Canada-sized collection is located on a National Library of Canada Gopher under the entries National Library of Canada Gopher Server and Canadian Government Information. It is available in English and French.

If you are using a Web browser, you don't have to step through the menu entries but can go directly to the collection. Use the following URL:

gopher://gopher.nlc-bnc.ca:70/11gopher$root%3a%5benglish%5d

What you'll find here is a huge amount of information about and from the federal Canadian government and six of the provincial governments. Under the Government Information entry, you'll find anything from the words of the national anthem to the Charter of Rights and Freedoms and subsequent constitutional accords, from Telnet links to government libraries. The range is just as broad if you look through the information about the federal departments, agencies, and ministries—anything from transcripts and schedules of the Canadian Broadcasting Corporation to an index of recent awards made by the Health Ministry (Figure 2.36). And this doesn't even begin to touch the information available from the provinces.

If you are looking for Canadian government information you should consider looking here. The only drawback is that there is no search facility available (and there is so much here that it's hard to know when to stop looking if you can't find what you want right away).

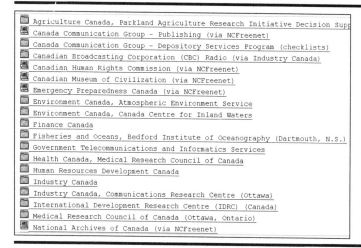

Agriculture Canada, Parkland Agriculture Research Initiative Decision Sup
Canada Communication Group - Publishing (via NCFreenet)
Canada Communication Group - Depository Services Program (checklists)
Canadian Broadcasting Corporation (CBC) Radio (via Industry Canada)
Canadian Human Rights Commission (via NCFreenet)
Canadian Museum of Civilization (via NCFreenet)
Emergency Preparedness Canada (via NCFreenet)
Environment Canada, Atmospheric Environment Service
Environment Canada, Canada Centre for Inland Waters
Finance Canada
Fisheries and Oceans, Bedford Institute of Oceanography (Dartmouth, N.S.)
Government Telecommunications and Informatics Services
Health Canada, Medical Research Council of Canada
Human Resources Development Canada
Industry Canada
Industry Canada, Communications Research Centre (Ottawa)
International Development Research Centre (IDRC) (Canada)
Medical Research Council of Canada (Ottawa, Ontario)
National Archives of Canada (via NCFreenet)

Figure 2.36:
Just some of the information about the Canadian federal government available from the Government of Canada Gopher

Laws of Other Nations

http://www.pls.com:8001/d2/kelli/httpd/htdocs/his/52.GBM

This Web page, part of the House of Representatives Internet Law Library, is a list of links to legal resources about (and sometimes in) seventy or so countries around the world.

The resources that the links in this list take you to would be described by a friend of mine as "mixed pickles." That is, the mix is so odd that it's fun to cruise and see what you find but it really isn't useful for research or reference purposes. For example, there is only a single article available for Vietnam on that country's recent economic development, while for England you'll find multiple copies of the Magna Charta, a copy of Prime Minister Chamberlain's speech before the House of Commons on the German invasion of Poland in 1939, a few miscellaneous articles, and the archives of a list mailing on European law. If this interests you, you might have some fun taking a short look around.

The Supreme Court of Canada

http://www.droit.umontreal.ca/CSC.html

This site is a collaborative effort between the Supreme Court of Canada and the Centre de Recherche en Droit Public at the University of Montreal

(Figure 2.37). You'll find the full text of opinions issued by the Supreme Court of Canada in cases from 1993 to the present. Some but not all 1992 opinions are also available.

The opinions are listed chronologically and you can search for them by key terms using WAIS search functions, which generally is a very useful way of finding the opinion you want. All opinions are bilingual English/French and are available for download in ASCII, WordPerfect 5.1 for DOS, and Word for the Macintosh formats.

Université de Montréal   Centre de recherche en droit public

The Supreme Court of Canada

This experimental service is brought to you thanks to a joint project between the **Supreme Court of Canada** and the **Centre de Recherche en Droit Public** at University of Montreal.

The **Supreme Court rulings** are available from 1993 and are in various formats.

You can also **search the Supreme Court database** using keywords.

You are the 34101 th visitor since July 15, 1994.

Figure 2.37:
The Supreme Court of Canada page, showing a picture of the court and links to its decisions

World Constitutions

http://www.econ.uni-hamburg.de/law/

World Constitutions is something of a misnomer for this site that lists 34 current and former countries (you'll find the U.S.S.R. constitution here). Yes, you will find the full text of the constitution for each country listed. You will also find a long list of facts and figures for each country. This is the kind of information you'd find in an almanac or the *CIA World Factbook*—you'll find at this site information on the population, ethnic groups, languages spoken, type of government, political parties represented in parliament, even a map of the world with the selected country highlighted. *World Constitutions* only begins to describe what you'll find here.

I enjoy reading the constitutions of other nations for the sake of comparison with our own and for what they say about a country's politics. The new South African constitution, for example, contains a guarantee of equal protection of the laws that prohibits discrimination on the basis of sexual orientation, among many other bases. Our equal protection clause has not been interpreted this way. China's constitution is an interesting read: it makes explicit territorial claims upon Taiwan. Whatever your reasons, if you need a constitution, take a look here.

 This site is located in Hamburg, Germany, so data transmission to the United States is often slow.

International Law

International law refers to the body of laws that govern the legal relations between nations. In this section you'll find a lot of United Nations information and also a good deal of international and multilateral treaties (full text).

If you are looking for sites on the laws of individual countries other than the U.S., see my "Laws of Other Nations" section, above.

DIANA: An International Human Rights Database

http://www.law.uc.edu/Diana

This site, located at the University of Cincinnati College of Law, is named for the late Professor Diana Vincent-Daviss, a renowned law librarian and bibliographer of the literature of human rights (Figure 2.38).

DIANA is noticeably under construction, but when complete it should be an excellent resource. It now contains (and hopefully will soon contain more) primary and secondary materials on international human rights. The primary sources contain a list of United Nations treaties, such as the Convention on Prevention and Punishment of Genocide, a list of documents from the Organization of American States, and decisions of the Inter-American Court of Human Rights. The secondary sources contain bibliographies and the full text of Professor Vincent-Daviss's own research guide.

The full text of the United Nations information is available elsewhere on the Internet. See the entries for The Multilaterals Project site and for The United Nations, later in this section.

DIANA

An International Human Rights Database

Dedicated to completing the pioneering work in human rights information of Diana Vincent-Daviss

The DIANA project is grateful for the generous support of the Ohio Board of Regents, the National Center for Automated Information Research and the United States Institute for Peace.

Primary Human Rights Sources

Secondary Human Rights Sources

Press here for a link to the Law School Constitutional Repository at the University of the Witwatersrand, Johannesburg, South Africa. Among the materials of interest at this site are the opinions in the recent death penalty case.

DIANA is an on-line resource inspired by the life and work of Professor Diana Vincent-Daviss, the late Deputy Director of the Orville H. Schell, Jr. Center for International Human Rights and librarian of Yale Law School. Professor Vincent-Daviss was a comprehensive bibliographer of literature on human rights. This service is named DIANA in her honor. DIANA has been established by the Schell Center, the Urban Morgan Institute for Human Rights, the Center for Electronic Text in the Law, the Yale Law Library and the University of Cincinnati College of Law Library. DIANA is designed to promote the creation,

Figure 2.38:
The home page for
DIANA: An
International Human
Rights Database.
DIANA is named for
the late professor and
librarian Diana Vincent-
Daviss.

The General Agreement on Tariffs and Trade (GATT 1994)

http://ananse.irv.uit.no/trade_law/gatt/nav/toc.html

This site, from the International Trade Law Project at the University of Tramsø in Norway, brings you the full text of GATT 1994, the General Agreement on Tariffs and Trade.

Lawyers should note that the copy of GATT available here is unofficial.

The text of GATT is quite large—some 100 kilobytes in total—and you are often handicapped here somewhat by slow data transmission from Norway. Another limitation is that the GATT is not searchable, so it is really only useful as a reference if you are already familiar with the text. Of course, if you just enjoy reading international treaties, you won't have a problem.

If the access time is really slow, there is a copy of GATT on a Gopher in the U.S., which is much faster to access, at the URL:

gopher://cyfer.esusda.gov/11/ace/policy/gatt

The Global Legal Studies Journal

http://www.law.indiana.edu/glsj/glsj.html

The *Global Legal Studies Journal* is a publication of the Indiana University School of Law, which makes the full text of the journal available electronically at this site. I include it here both because of the breadth of its subject matter and because there aren't that many full-text journals on the Internet.

If you are looking for other law journals on line (full text or not), see the Online Law Journals and Periodicals entry under the "Best 'Smorgasboard Sites': Sites with Everything!" heading of my section "Have a Problem? Check Here First!"

The *Journal*'s subject matter isn't international law per se. Rather, it is concerned with the interactions between and among international, national, and local laws, politics, and culture. An entire recent issue, for example, contains many articles on different aspects of international migration. Representative articles from another issue are: "European Integration: Reflections on Its Limits and Effects" and "The U.S.-Japan Trading Relationship and Its Effects."

The *Journal* is a recent creation, so there are three full-text issues available as of this writing, with more to come. If this subject interests you, it is nice to have such a resource available on line.

The Multilaterals Project

http://www.tufts.edu/departments/fletcher/multilaterals.html

The *Multilaterals Project* comes from the Fletcher School of Law & Diplomacy at Tufts University. The *Project*'s purpose is to "make available the texts of international multilateral conventions and other instruments"—such as international treaties from the United Nations and other bodies—and it succeeds quite well.

You'll find treaties on a broad range of subjects: "the atmosphere and space," "biodiversity," "cultural protection," "human rights," and more, all the way down alphabetically to "warfare and arms control" (Figure 2.39). All the major treaties are here: The Geneva Conventions, the Maastricht Treaty on European Union, and the Convention on the Prevention and Punishment of Genocide.

Better still, the full text of the treaties can be searched. My only regret is that the signatory countries to each treaty aren't listed anywhere. That's something that would be nice to know.

 The treaties in the *Project*'s collection are available for download in ASCII and WordPerfect format from the Fletcher School's FTP site at the following URL:

ftp.fletcher.tufts.edu

in the /pub/diplomacy directory. The file names are numerical, so you must first consult the Index file to find the file name for the treaty you want.

Multilaterals Project
@ The Fletcher School of Law & Diplomacy

About the Multilaterals Project

Multilateral Conventions organized by subject

    Atmosphere and Space
    Flora and Fauna -- Biodiversity
    Cultural Protection
    Diplomatic Relations
    General
    Human Rights
    Marine and Coastal
    Other Environmental
    Trade and Commercial Relations
    Rules of Warfare; Arms Control

Chronological listing of conventions and other instruments in the order of the date of signature.

Search the text files of the Multilaterals Project:

Unselect this to search partial words too (it's much slower): ☒
Enter search text: [   ] [Submit]

Figure 2.39:
The Multilaterals Project. Links to international conventions are organized by subject.

The North American Free Trade Agreement (NAFTA)

Niord.SHSU.edu

This full-text copy of the North American Free Trade Agreement is available on a Sam Houston State University Gopher under the entries Economics (SHSU Network Access Initiative Project) and NAFTA (North American Free Trade Agreement).

If you are using a Web browser, you can go right to NAFTA with the URL:

gopher://Niord.SHSU.edu/11gopher_root%3a%5b_DATA.NAFTA%5D

NAFTA as presented here is well organized. There is a table of contents and a synopsis and the full text of the agreement is broken down into its component chapters. It is searchable, which is important given the large size of the agreement. If you need a copy of NAFTA as a reference, you should check in here.

NAFTA is a fairly popular Internet item; you can find links to copies at a number of sites at a University of Nevada-Reno Gopher:

futique.scs.unr.edu

under the entries Selected Information Resources by Topic, Government and Politics, and NAFTA.

To access the above sites directly by Web browser, use the URL:

gopher://futique.scs.unr.edu:70/11/Selected/Government/NAFTA

The United Nations Crime and Justice Information Network

uacsc2.albany.edu

The United Nations Crime and Justice Information Network was established in 1989, admittedly on a limited budget, "to establish a world wide network to enhance dissemination and the exchange of information concerning criminal justice and crime prevention issues." The network is located on a State University of New York at Albany Gopher under the entry United Nations Justice Network.

The collection here is diverse, as you might guess from the mandate. You'll find UN rules on criminal justice, including such things as model treaties on extradition and mutual assistance in criminal matters, and safeguards guaranteeing protection of rights for prisoners facing the death penalty. You'll also find raw data on crimes and criminal prosecutions in countries around the world, and links to related networks and to criminal justice agency information.

The United Nations

nywork1.undp.org

This Gopher site contains a wealth of information about the United Nations. You'll find information about the UN itself—what it is and what it does. For example, there is a copy of the UN Charter and an organization chart, and information about UN special agencies such as UNICEF (the United Nations Children's Fund) and the International Court of Justice located in the Hague. You'll even find information on all current UN peacekeeping operations (there are more than you might think—see Figure 2.40).

In a similar vein, there are press releases and official publications from UN-sponsored world conferences. You'll find, for example, such information from the 1994 World Conference on Natural Disaster Reduction and from the 1995 Fourth World Conference on Women.

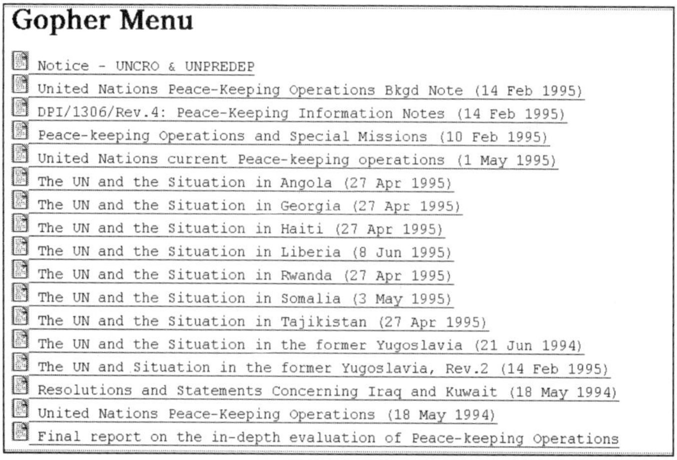

Gopher Menu

- Notice - UNCRO & UNPREDEP
- United Nations Peace-Keeping Operations Bkgd Note (14 Feb 1995)
- DPI/1306/Rev.4: Peace-Keeping Information Notes (14 Feb 1995)
- Peace-keeping Operations and Special Missions (10 Feb 1995)
- United Nations current Peace-keeping operations (1 May 1995)
- The UN and the Situation in Angola (27 Apr 1995)
- The UN and the Situation in Georgia (27 Apr 1995)
- The UN and the Situation in Haiti (27 Apr 1995)
- The UN and the Situation in Liberia (8 Jun 1995)
- The UN and the Situation in Rwanda (27 Apr 1995)
- The UN and the Situation in Somalia (3 May 1995)
- The UN and the Situation in Tajikistan (27 Apr 1995)
- The UN and the Situation in the former Yugoslavia (21 Jun 1994)
- The UN and Situation in the former Yugoslavia, Rev.2 (14 Feb 1995)
- Resolutions and Statements Concerning Iraq and Kuwait (18 May 1994)
- United Nations Peace-Keeping Operations (18 May 1994)
- Final report on the in-depth evaluation of Peace-keeping Operations

Figure 2.40:
Information from the
United Nations Gopher
on UN peacekeeping
operations

Finally, and I found this most interesting, there is the full text of UN General Assembly resolutions dating from the 36th Session (1981) and of Security Council resolutions from 1974. If you want or need UN information, this is the place to go.

The World Intellectual Property Organization

http://www.uspto.gov/wipo.html

This Web page for the World Intellectual Property Organization (WIPO, pronounced "wipe-o") is actually part of the United States Patent and Trademark Office Web site. WIPO is a UN agency whose purpose is the "promotion of the protection of intellectual property throughout the world through cooperation among States and...the administration of...the legal and administrative aspects of intellectual property."

Unfortunately, the information available here is limited. You'll find links to the text of a small number of international intellectual property conventions, such as the Bern Convention for Protection of Literary and

Famous Supreme Court Cases: New York Times v. Sullivan

Sullivan was an elected Commissioner of Birmingham, Alabama. He sued the New York Times for libel for an advertisement it ran in March 1960 about the civil rights movement in the South. A jury awarded Sullivan $500,000 in damages. The Supreme Court reversed this judgment, holding that the First Amendment freedom to speak provides broad protection for the press to criticize the conduct of public officials.

The protection afforded by the First Amendment is broad indeed. Justice William Brennan wrote for the Court: "The constitutional guarantees require, we think, a federal rule that prohibits a public official from recovering damages for a defamatory falsehood relating to his official conduct unless he proves that the statement was made with 'actual malice'—that is, with knowledge that it was false or with reckless disregard of whether it was false or not...."

Artistic Works and the Universal Copyright Convention. You'll also find intellectual property laws from various countries around the world—the Korean Patent Law and the Great Britain Registered Designs Act, for example.

More WIPO documents do exist, but the organization has not made them widely available, preferring instead to sell them, and only upon request. Ordering information is available on this Web page.

Best Ways of Finding More and Better Sites

The Internet is so large and is growing so quickly that at some point somewhere along the line, you're going to want to find something and not know where to look. Maybe you'll want information on a law subject not covered in this book or maybe you'll want something else entirely. Friends will be able to help you out some of the time, but what you really need is the Internet equivalent of Directory Assistance or, better yet, a crack reference librarian.

Many of the sites mentioned in this book have built-in search programs that allow you to search through the data at that particular site. This section's search programs cast a much wider net. For example, some of the programs described here allow you to search the World Wide Web. One of the programs, Veronica, allows you to seach all of Gopherspace. The search programs here are valuable tools for tracking down whatever interests you.

Collected Search Engines

http://oneworld.wa.com/htmldev/devpage/search.html

This page comes from an organization called Oneworld Information Services. As of this writing it has a list of links to 33 different search programs, and new ones are added frequently.

Some of the search programs listed are devoted to a specific subject. For example, there's one that lets you search for Mac software, another for shareware, and another for computer programming language resources. A few programs are just for searching a particular reference like the *CIA World Fact Book* and the *Big Dummy's Guide to the Internet*.

The remaining search programs search the Internet generally. This list includes links to *Veronica*, *WebCrawler*, and *The World Wide Web Worm*, each of which I discuss in more detail below. Try these search programs and some others. When you find one that works well, or a few that work well together, stick with them. When you need a search program, this is the place to look.

Veronica

veronica.scs.unr.edu

If you want to search for something on a Gopher, Veronica is the way to go.

Veronica, which, somewhat incredibly, stands for "Very Easy Rodent-Oriented Net-wide Index of Computerized Archives" allows you to search Gopherspace—all the Gopher servers in the world! In your search you may end up going from one Veronica to another. This Veronica access site is on a Gopher at the University of Nevada-Reno under the menu entry Search ALL of GopherSpace using Veronica.

If you're using a Web browser, you can go directly to this Veronica by using the URL:

gopher://veronica.scs.unr.edu/11/veronica

What you'll find here is a list of links to active Veronicas around the world, from NYSERnet in New York State to the University of Pisa in Italy and beyond (see Figure 2.41). Any one of them allows you to do a key terms search of Gopherspace in two different ways. The more thorough way is through Search GopherSpace by Title word. This kind of search will return every single "resource" whose title contains the key terms you enter (a resource can be anything from an ASCII file to a graphics file to another Gopher). If searching this way buries you in information, and it might, try searching ONLY DIRECTORIES by Title word, which only searches the names of Gopher directories.

Although your Veronica search may be faster if you choose the Veronica nearest you, Veronicas are often overloaded, so you may find you get your best results with one halfway around the world! If you use Veronica enough, you'll get a sense of which ones are faster, and when.

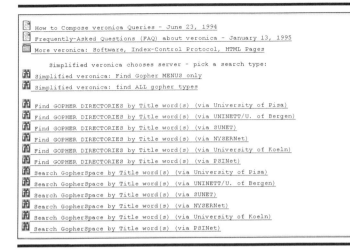

Figure 2.41:
Veronicas around the world allow you to search Gopherspace.

Almost every Gopher server will have an entry that gives you access to Veronica. If the Veronica via your Gopher site is unavailable, try it from the "top-level" Gopher at the University of Minnesota, at:

gopher://gopher.tc.umn.edu/11/Other%20Gopher%20and%20Information%20Servers/Veronica

WebCrawler

http://webcrawler.cs.washington.edu/WebCrawler/WebQuery.html

Because WebCrawler is so easy and works well, I would recommend beginning your searches on the Web here. If you want to expand your searches, use WebCrawler together with The World Wide Web Worm (the entry following this one), or go all out and widen your search even further using Lycos (the final entry).

WebCrawler is brought to you by America Online, though they did not invent it. WebCrawler allows you to do a key terms search on over 100,000 documents (i.e., pages) on the World Wide Web. Now this is by no means all of the pages out there, but it is a good sample. What makes WebCrawler nice, though, is that it searches the full text of these 100,000 pages and it is very easy to use.

WebCrawler does only two kinds of searches, an AND search and an OR search. An AND search will only find pages that contain *all* of the key terms you search for. To do an AND search, turn on the **AND words together** option. An OR search will find pages that contain any one or more of the key terms you search for.

If WebCrawler says there are no matches for your search, you may be doing an AND search with too many search terms. Try using fewer terms or doing an OR search.

The World Wide Web Worm

http://www.cs.colorado.edu/home/mcbryan/WWWW.html

The World Wide Web Worm is an excellent Web search program (as shown in Figure 2.42). I find that it works well when I use it together with WebCrawler (above), since they search in different ways. Where WebCrawler searches only the text of Web pages, the Worm can search for four different things:

◆ URLs (use the **Search Only in Document Addresses** option)

◆ Page Titles (use the **Search Only in Document Titles** option)

◆ The links on Web pages (use the **Search All URL References** option)

◆ The URLs in the links on Web pages (use the **Search all URL Addresses** option)

WWWW - WORLD WIDE WEB WORM

Best of the Web '94 - Best Navigational Aid. Oliver McBryan

Serving 3,000,000 URL's to 2,000,000 folks/month.
Instructions, Definitions, Examples, Failures, Register, WWWW Paper.
Last Run: April 15

1. Search all URL references

a. AND - match all keywords
b. OR - match any keyword   5 matches

Keywords:

Start Search

Figure 2.42:
The World Wide Web Worm, a search program for the WWW

With the Worm and WebCrawler together, you can find what you're looking for pretty quickly.

Lycos

http://lycos.cs.cmu.edu

In addition to the WebCrawler and World Wide Web Worm above, there are many other good search programs available on the Internet. Lycos, from Carnegie Mellon University in Pittsburgh, is one of the most extensive such programs out there, allowing you to search nearly 4.5 million Web pages!

Like other search programs, Lycos lets you search by key words, and returns links to documents that match the words you're searching for. In addition, Lycos gives you the title and a summary of the pages that match your query. This will save you some time, because it allows you to see right away which pages you want and which ones you don't.

In addition to searching for a list of key words, Lycos allows you to compose complex queries. It doesn't use standard WAIS syntax, but this is not a problem, because the online help for Lycos is quite good.

WAIS Searches

Many of the search programs at the sites in this book allow you to do WAIS (Wide Area Information Service) searches. Essentially the way this works is that first someone has already indexed all of the words in the documents you can search through. The indexed documents may be relatively few and may all be located at one site, or they may be many and located all across the Internet. Then when you enter your key terms, WAIS checks the index for these words and presents links to any document that contains them.

What's nice about WAIS is that you have a number of different *logical functions* that you can use to refine your search. Here's how they work:

AND   If you search for "bias" AND "prejudice" the search will return only those documents that contain both terms.

OR   If you search for "bias" OR "prejudice" the search will return documents that contain one or both of these terms.

NOT   If you search for "bias" NOT "prejudice" the search will return documents that contain "bias" but do not contain "prejudice."

*   The asterisk is used just like the DOS wildcard asterisk character. If you search for "prejud*" the search will return any document that contains "prejudice" or "prejudicial" or any other term beginning with "prejud."

These logical functions can all be combined (and with a little practice, you can become an expert at composing searches). For example, you could run a search like "prior" AND "inconsistent" AND "statement" OR "impeac*", which would return:

1. documents containing all of the first three terms (but not words beginning with "impeac");

2. documents containing words like "impeach," "impeachment," or "impeaching" (but not the first three words);

3. *and* documents containing all of the first three terms and words beginning "impeac."

Finally, not every search program you come across will be the same. Some will give you more and some will give you fewer logical functions, while others are quite sophisticated and are written for a particular site (see, for example, the entry for the Code of Federal Regulations, under the heading "Laws, Codes, and Rules" in my "Lawyer's Desk Reference" section earlier in Part Two). The basic WAIS functions will usually serve you well, though, and online help is usually available.

Appendices

Where Do I Go from Here?

Now that you know the basics and what's out there on the Internet, you may want to find out more about using the Internet. For example, you may want to learn in more detail about the World Wide Web, Usenet, Gopher, and FTP, *and* the software and tools you can use to make the most of your Internet travels.

If you'd like a basic, plain English tour of the Internet and its uses, then *Easy Guide to the Internet* by Christian Crumlish is for you. It's like having an Internet guru at your side, explaining everything as you go along. Another great book for newbies is *Access the Internet* by David Peal. This book even includes NetCruiser software, which will get you connected via an easy point-and-click interface in no time.

For an introduction to the World Wide Web, turn to *Surfing the Internet with Netscape* or *Mosaic Access to the Internet*, both by Daniel A. Tauber and Brenda Kienan. Each of these books walks you through getting connected, and they both include the software you need to get started on the Web in a jiffy.

For quick and easy Internet reference, turn to the *Internet Instant Reference* by Paul Hoffman, and for an in-depth overview, try the best-selling *Internet Roadmap* by Bennett Falk. To get familiar with the lingo, you can turn to the compact and concise *Internet Dictionary* by Christian Crumlish.

If you've just got to learn all there is to know about the Internet, the comprehensive, complete *Mastering the Internet* by Glee Harrah Cady and Pat McGregor is for you. And if you want to find out what tools and utilities are available (often on the Internet itself) to maximize the power of your Internet experience, you'll want to check out *The Internet Tool Kit* by Nancy Cedeno.

All of these books have been published by Sybex.

Internet Service Providers

If you need to set up an account with an Internet service provider, this is the place for you. This appendix lists providers in the United States, Canada, Great Britain, Ireland, Australia, and New Zealand.

The service providers listed here offer full Internet service, including SLIP/PPP accounts, which allow you to use Web browsers like Mosaic and Netscape.

The list we're providing here is by no means comprehensive. We're concentrating on service providers that offer national or nearly national Internet service in English-speaking countries. You may prefer to go with a service provider that's local to your area—to minimize your phone bill, it is important to find a service provider that offers a local or toll-free phone number for access.

When you inquire into establishing an account with any of the providers listed in this appendix tell them the type of account you want—you may want a shell account, if you know and plan to use Unix commands to get around, or you may want the type of point-and-click access that's offered through Netcom's NetCruiser. If you want to run a Web browser like Mosaic or Netscape, you must have a SLIP or PPP account. Selecting an Internet service provider is a matter of personal preference and local access. Shop around, and if you aren't satisfied at any point, change providers.

When you're shopping around for an Internet service provider, the most important questions to ask are (a) "What is the nearest local access number?" and (b) "What are the monthly service charges and is there a setup (or registration) fee?"

What's Out There

Three very good sources of information about Internet service providers are available on the Internet itself. Peter Kaminski's Public Dialup Internet Access list (PDIAL) is at

ftp://ftp.netcom.com/pub/in/info-deli/public-access/pdial.

Yahoo's Internet Access Providers list is at

http://www.yahoo.com/Business/COrporations/Internet_Access_providers/.

CyberSpace Today's list is at

http://www.cybertoday.com/.

IN THE UNITED STATES

In this section we list Internet service providers that provide local access phone numbers in most major American cities. These are the big, national companies. Many areas also have smaller regional Internet providers, which may offer better local access if you're not in a big city. You can find out about these smaller companies by looking in local computer papers like *MicroTimes* or *Computer Currents* or by getting on the Internet via one of these big companies and checking out the Peter Kaminski, Yahoo, and Cyberspace Today service provider listings.

Opening an account with any of the providers listed here will get you full access to the World Wide Web, and full-fledged e-mail service (allowing you to send and receive e-mail). You'll also get the ability to read and post articles to Usenet newsgroups.

Netcom

Netcom Online Communications Services is a national Internet service provider with local access numbers in most major cities. As of this writing, they have over 100 local access numbers in the United States and an 800 access number for those who don't live near the local access numbers. Using the 800 number invloves an additional fee. Netcom's NetCruiser software gives you point-and-click access to the Internet. (Netcom also provides a shell account, but stay away from it if you want to run Netscape.) Starting with NetCruiser version 1.6, it is possible to run Netscape on top of NetCruiser. Especially for beginning users who want a point-and-click interface and easy setup of Netscape, this may be a good choice

NetCruiser software is available on disk for free but without documentation at many trade shows and bookstores. It is also available with a very good book (*Access the Internet, Second Edition*; David Peal, Sybex, 1996) that shows you how to use the software. To contact Netcom directly, phone (800) 353-6600 or fax (408) 241-9145.

Performance Systems International (PSINet)

Performance Systems International is a national Internet Service Provider with local access numbers in many American cities *and in Japan*. These folks are currently upgrading their modems to 28.8Kbps, which will give you faster access to the Internet.

To contact PSI directly, phone (800) 82P-SI82 or fax 800-FAXPSI-1.

UUNet/AlterNet

UUNet Technologies and AlterNet offer Internet service throughout the United States. They run their own national network.

You can contact UUNet and AlterNet by phone at (800) 488-6383 or by fax at (703)-206-5601.

Portal

Portal Communications, Inc., an Internet Service Provider located in the San Francisco Bay Area, lets you get connected either by dialing one of their San Francisco Bay Area phone numbers or via the CompuServe network. (This is not CompuServe Information Services, but rather the network on which CompuServe runs.) The CompuServe network, with over 400 access phone numbers, is a local call from most of the United States.

You can contact Portal by phone at (408) 973-9111 or by fax at (408)-752-1580.

IN CANADA

Listed here are providers that offer access to Internet service in the areas around large Canadian cities. For information about local access in less populated regions, get connected and check out the Peter Kaminski, Yahoo, and Cyberspace Today lists described earlier in this appendix.

 Many Internet service providers in the U.S. also offer service in Canada and in border towns near Canada. If you're interested and you're in Canada, you can ask some of the big American service providers whether they have a local number near you.

UUNet Canada

UUNet Canada is the Canadian division of the United States service provider UUNet/AlterNet, which we described earlier in this chapter. UUNet Canada offers Internet service to large portions of Canada.

You can contact UUNet Canada directly by phoning (416) 368-6621 or by fax at (416) 368-1350.

Internet Direct

Internet Direct offers access to folks in the Toronto and Vancouver areas.

You can contact Internet Direct by phoning (604) 691-1600 or faxing (604) 691-1605

IN GREAT BRITAIN AND IRELAND

The Internet is, after all, international. Here are some service providers located and offering service in Great Britain and Ireland.

UNet

Located in the northwest part of England, with more locations promised, UNet offers access at speeds up to 28.8K along with various Internet tools for your use.

They can be reached by phone at 0925 633 144.

Easynet

London-based Easynet provides Internet service throughout England via Pipex, along with a host of Internet tools.

You can reach them by phone at 0171 209 0990.

Ireland On-Line

Serving most (if not all) of Ireland, including Belfast, Ireland On-Line offers complete Internet service including ISDN and leased-line connections.

Contact Ireland On-Line by phone at 00 353 (0)1 8551740.

IN AUSTRALIA AND NEW ZEALAND

Down under in Australia and New Zealand the Internet is as happening as it is in the northern hemisphere; many terrific sites are located in Australia especially. Here are a couple of service providers for that part of the world.

Connect.com.au

In wild and woolly Australia, Internet service (SLIP/PPP) is available from Connect.com.au Pty Ltd.

You can contact the people at Connect.com.au by phone at 61 3 528 2239.

Actrix

Actrix Information Exchange offers Internet service (PPP accounts) in the Wellington, New Zealand area.

You can reach these folks by phone at 64 4 389 6316.

Index

Note to the Reader: Throughout this index **boldfaced** page numbers indicate primary discussions of a topic. *Italicized* page numbers indicate illustrations.

forms

readers for, **68**

from Social Security Administration, 68

tax, 70, *71*

for trademark applications, 55–56

Fourteenth Amendment, 75

Freedom of Information Act guide, 66

freedom of speech case, **80**

Frequently Asked Questions (FAQs), 31

FTP (File Transfer Protocol), **15–16**, 32, 88

Full-Text Patent Searches, 52

Full-Text Patent Searches II, 53

G

General Agreement on Tariffs and Trade (GATT 1994), 145

General Assembly resolutions, 150

Gideon v. Wainright, **94–95**

Global Arbitration Mediation Association, Inc., 101

Global Legal Studies Journal, 146

Gophers, **12–13**, 153–154, *154*

.gov domain, 4

government, **85–86**

Canadian, 138–140, *139*, *141*

Federal. *See* Federal government

state, **127–135**

Government of Canada, 140, *141*

graphics, 8, 25, *25*

Great Britain, Internet service providers in, 163–164

Green Page, 60

H

handbook of U.S. government, 114–115

Harlan, John Marshall, 80

Hermes Project, 91–92

home pages, 9

House of Commons, 138

House of Representatives gopher, 122

House of Representatives Internet Law Library, 82–83, *83*

for Code of Federal Regulations, 96

for fundamental documents, 40

for law libraries, 111

House of Representatives web page, 122–123

.html (Hypertext Markup Language) suffix, 11

HTTP (Hypertext Transfer Protocol), 11

human rights database, 9, *9*, 144, *145*

humor, 30

hyperlinks, 10

Hypertext Markup Language (.html) suffix, 11

Hypertext Transfer Protocol (HTTP), 11

I

immigration law, **61–63**

indexes

subject, 80–81, *81*

topical law, 86

Indiana Code, 131

Indiana State Bills, 132

information providers. *See* access providers

T

U

V

Now available wherever computer books are sold.

Internet surfing... for kids only.

This extraordinary, interactive, easy-to-use book lets kids access the world of the Internet from the keyboard of their PC or Mac. The  **companion disk provides a special "kids version" of NetCruiser®, the popular Web browser, and waives the usual $25 registration fee!**

Internet for Kids

Deneen Frazier
with Dr. Barbara Kurshan and Dr. Sara Armstrong

Explore
the World
Step-by-S
with Hand
Activities

With a
by U.S
Bob K

Custom
Pushbu
NetCrui
Software
Kids Inst
Internet A

315 pages   ISBN 1741-4

SYBEX Inc. • 2021 Challenger Dr., Alameda, CA 94501 • 800-227-2346 • 510-523-8233

Quick fixes and fast facts.

SECOND EDITION

The **Internet** INSTANT REFERENCE

▶ Updated Coverage of Tools, Resources, and Commands

▶ Concise, Plain-English Answers from A to Z

▶ For All Skill Levels— Beginner to Expert

Paul E. Hoffman

SYBEX

Covers Mosaic, Netscape, and the World Wide Web

Y ou'll value the convenience, speed and thoroughness of the Second Edition of the book rated "the most comprehensive Internet reference available" when it comes to covering the fast-changing Internet. You'll find the latest on connection software, browsers, terminology, and online resources.

Now available wherever computer books are sold.

SYBEX Inc.
2021 Challenger Dr.
Alameda, CA 94501
800-227-2346
510-523-8233

346 pages   ISBN 1719-8

SYBEX

⌂ SYBEX · NEW · ⌂ SYBEX · HOT!

Roadmaps for Travelers on the Information Superhighway

The Pocket Tour™ Series

What's your interest?

Sports? Games? Music? Travel?
Money? Health and Fitness?
Whatever it is, the Internet's
crammed with everything you
could ever want to know on
the subject.

Knowing where to look, however, is
another matter. That's why Sybex
has developed the exclusive Pocket
Tour™ series—to guide
you every step of the way through
the often confusing Internet maze.

Watch for additional
Sybex Pocket Tours of:

- *Celebrities*
- *Food & Drink*
- *Kidstuff*
- *Law*
- *Shopping*

SYBEX

Games	Health & Fitness	Money	Music	Sports	Travel
1694-9	1711-2	1696-5	1695-7	1693-0	1760-0

The Complete Pocket Tour Series from Sybex

A Pocket Tour of:

Food & Drink on the Internet

Games on the Internet

Health & Fitness on the Internet

Kidstuff on the Internet

Law on the Internet

Money on the Internet

Music on the Internet

Shopping on the Internet

Sports on the Internet

Travel on the Internet

with more coming soon to a store near you.